TONY BENN

TONY BENN

A CRITICAL BIOGRAPHY BY RUSSELL LEWIS

ASSOCIATED BUSINESS PRESS

LONDON

Published by Associated Business Press
An imprint of Associated Business Programmes Limited
Ludgate House
107-111 Fleet Street
London EC4A 2AB

First published 1978

© copyright Russell Lewis 1978

ISBN 0 85227 211 1

Typeset by Photographics, Stockland,
Nr. Honiton, Devon
Printed and bound in Great Britain by Redwood Burn Ltd., Trowbridge and Esher.

TO MY BROTHER JOHN

CONTENTS

A CHRONOLOGY OF EVENTS

1925   Born 3 April, son of William Wedgwood Benn MP.

1926   General Strike.

1929   Ramsay Macdonald's second Labour government. William Wedgwood Benn appointed Secretary of State for India.

1939   War declared.

1941   Benn's father created Viscount Stansgate.

1942   Benn first goes to New College, Oxford.

1943   He joins the Labour party.
        He joins the Royal Air Force.

1945   Labour landslide; Atlee forms Government.

1946   Returns to Oxford; becomes President of the Union; goes on speaking tour to USA.

1949   Marries Caroline Middleton de Camp, daughter of
        well-to-do Cincinnati businessman.
        Joins BBC; becomes producer, North America
        Service.

1950   First elected MP for Bristol South-East.

1951   Labour government falls; Churchill returns to
        power.

1956   Benn is founder member of Campaign for Nuclear
        Disarmament and of Movement for Colonial
        Freedom.

1957   Publishes Fabian pamphlet advocating that the Privy
        Council should replace the House of Lords as second
        chamber. Ironically tipped to become Labour leader
        in the Lords.

1959   Macmillan's 'You never had it so good' election
        triumph.
        Benn first elected to Labour's National Executive.

1960   Benn leaves Gaitskell camp and goes over to Wilson.
        Lord Stansgate dies; Benn's campaign to renounce
        title begins.

1961   Parliamentary Committee of Privileges turns down
        Benn's plea to renounce peerage. He stands for
        Parliament in by-election, wins but is barred from
        entering Commons.

1963   Bill to allow peers to renounce titles passes through
        Parliament. Benn re-elected.

1964   Benn becomes Chairman of Fabian Society and of
        Labour's advisory committee on broadcasting.

Wilson's narrow victory at general election. Benn appointed Postmaster General.

1966   Labour wins second general election. Benn appointed Minister of Technology after Frank Cousins resigns.

1967   Collapse of National Plan.
        Wilson's application to join EEC vetoed by General de Gaulle.

1968   Benn as Minister of Technology announces Concorde development bill is five times original estimate.

1969   Upper Clyde Shipbuilders crisis; bye-election in Glasgow; Benn bails out UCS.

1970   Conservative victory in general election; Heath becomes Prime Minister.

1971   Benn addresses 50 000-strong rally in Glasgow against closure of UCS.

1972   Benn is Chairman of the Labour party.

1973   Labour party conference votes for Benn's scheme for wholesale nationalisation.

1974   Miners' strike.
        Labour wins February general election; Benn becomes Secretary of State for Industry.
        Court Line affair.
        October general election; Labour returned with increased majority.

1975   Benn is Chairman of Labour party home policy committee.
        Industry Act passed.

Referendum vote two to one in favour of staying in the Common Market.
Benn transferred to Energy Ministry; first supplies of North Sea oil arrive in Britain.

1976   Wilson resigns; Benn stands for election as leader. Callaghan wins and becomes leader and Prime Minister. Benn retains Energy Ministry.
Benn wins clash with Callaghan over appointment of Andy Bevan.

1977   Further clashes with Callaghan and Healey over economic and pay policy, but Benn does not resign.

FOREWORD

Why have I written a book about Anthony Wedgwood Benn?
I was originally drawn to the idea three years ago when an
account of Tony Benn's career seemed a natural sequel and
complement to my then recently completed biography of
Margaret Thatcher, since these two politicians of opposite
persuasions — born in the same year and both shaped by
post-war Oxford — stand for the alternatives between which
the British people must choose. Mrs Thatcher represents to
the point of personification our people's best hope of
retaining the best of their ancient values and renewing their
national self-respect; Mr Benn is a remarkable embodiment
of the trends and forces which, if given the upper hand, will
render such restoration and renewal impossible. My
documentary pilgrimage through Mr Benn's political career,
which includes twenty-eight years of oration in Parliament,
has only confirmed my original melancholy impression that
if we really are destined to arrive in George Orwell's *1984* or
Constantine Fitzgibbon's Britain 'where the kissing has to
stop', Benn (I shall from now on for brevity's sake dispense
with the 'Mr') is the man to lead us there.

More than any other leading Labour politician Benn talks
of the need for 'fundamental and irreversible change' in our
society. Moreover, despite his talk of the urgent need for
popular participation in political decisions is he anxious that

such change shall come about through genuine consent? 'Comrades', he said to the 1972 Labour conference, 'the era of so-called "consensus" politics is over.' The final objective is of course socialism — the concentration of all economic as well as political power in state hands — to be realised as soon as maybe through the work of a single-chamber legislature, one of the many planks in the Benn platform being the abolition of the House of Lords.

Fortunately, Benn's grand design remains unfulfilled and in this country we still enjoy a democratic and free society. Because of the capitalist system, economic power — although now dangerously concentrated — is still sufficiently dispersed to sustain plenty of political independence, though whether it will survive the further assault from the deceptively mild-sounding 'industrial democracy' remains to be seen. In this context it is worth noting that nobody on the Labour front bench is so attached as Benn to workers' control — ominously, a term associated with the so-called workers' states of the Soviet bloc where the workers are of course more under the thumb of the bosses than anywhere else in the world. To Benn 'industrial democracy' is not just a fashionable phrase but a programme for advancing the power of the new boss class: the trades union heirarchy, which Benn cultivates more assiduously than even Michael Foot.

Benn's connections with worker militancy extend in other directions. He is demonstrably sympathetic with the Trotskyists of the Militant Tendency who have been infiltrating the Labour party constituency organisation, taking over management committees and either getting rid of the sitting Member (as in the notorious case of Reg Prentice at Newham North East) or making them conform to Trotskyite ideas. Similarly, Benn was responsible for keeping Andy Bevan, a well known Trotskyite Militant, in his job as Labour's National Youth Officer, even though this was contrary to the expressed wish of James Callaghan, Prime Minister and Labour leader.

Against this background it is not difficult to see something more than eccentricity and undergraduate enthusiasm in that collection of attitudes which have come to be known as 'Bennery', whose evolution I chronicle in the pages that follow: the irreversible changes, the workers' control, the censorship of the media, the attitudes to the law (Benn seems to believe that people such as the Clay Cross councillors and trades unionists in trouble with the police have a special dispensation to break the law with impunity).

However, it is not as an originator of extreme ideas that Benn is important, but as a tireless propagandist of them within the Labour party, especially in recent years after becoming Chairman of its home policy committee. It is not widely realised just how responsible Benn was for the extremist programme of nationalisation adopted by the Labour conference in 1976 — a policy more extreme than the platform on which the Italian Communist party stood at Italy's last general election — and workers' control needless to say figures prominently in the policy drafts which the home policy committee continually forms. Too little appreciated as well is how much Benn contributed to the eclipse of the social democratic wing of the Labour party in the Seventies. He skilfully — Benn is a consummate political tactician — used the Common Market issue to isolate the Social Democrats, making the position of Roy Jenkins in particular impossible and leading to the departure of Dick Taverne.

It is often suggested that Benn himself is isolated in the present Labour Cabinet and is a waning influence not to be taken seriously. In fact, he has cleverly stayed on in the Cabinet while at the same time making it clear that he is in disagreement with many of its policies, especially those connected with the IMF, requiring monetary continence, the reduction of public expenditure and the abandonment of fiscal follies like the wealth tax — Benn's view being that a crisis is the occasion not for slowing down but for speeding up the movement to socialism. Thus while other members of the front bench have as a matter of solidarity felt obliged to grin and bear policies which may be unpopular with some of their supporters, Benn is given credit by the Labour grassroots for the purity of his socialism. In this way he is using his position as Cabinet maverick to build up a nationwide constituency on the Left.

These thoughts on Benn are all the more seasonal in the light of the inevitable general election some time in Autumn 1978 or early 1979. As I try to show in this book, a vote for Callaghan then will mean a programme of Bennery and the subsequent emergence as leader of Benn himself. Needless to say, the issue is very differently presented by James Callaghan, who has done all he can to create a popular image of himself as a Labour version of Stanley Baldwin or even as an avuncular old Tory who just happens to be Labour Prime Minister. His appeal is indeed conservative of sorts — a plea for the preservation of the *status quo sine bellum,* for a continuation of the lull in legislative activity which has been with us since November 1976 when Labour lost its overall majority in the Commons and was at the same time pressured by the International Monetary Fund to desist from its more economically dangerous policies. As in 1969, the IMF has once more appeared as friendly neighbourhood creditor to insist that Labour's spendthrift ways be curbed, and Callaghan's election ploy is essentially that this tutelary regime is the best we can hope for, that change can only be for the worse and that indeed change under the Conservatives can only mean a renewal of the industrial strife which we escaped with the defeat of the last Tory government.

However, though it is often true in history that nothing lasts like the provisional, the Callaghan regime, even if it were the least of all possible evils, is vastly more provisional than most. A working Labour majority would mean a tilt to the left in the composition of the parliamentary Labour party and the immediate resumption of the legislative programme so happily stalled in the autumn of 1976. It is the imminent prospect of this programme, plus the very availability of Benn in the prime of life with remarkable demagogic gifts which makes it not merely a rhetorical, but a serious and objective, question whether the coming election may prove the last free election Britain has: although elections may have crucial role in the future — as indeed they have long had in the countries of the Soviet bloc — the changes wrought by Benn and his allies to the very structure of our economy and society would be so 'irreversible' that a ritual affirmation of one party dictatorship is all they could amount to.

Lastly, I would hope that this biography, if it is a tract for the times, can also claim some wider interest. The very ascent of such a politician as Benn tells us something about the kind of society which has allowed him to come to the fore. There is something worrying about an old and sophisticated community which can respond to what in many cases one can only call the ravings of a politician whose outlook is so manifestly consumed with guilt about the privileges of his origin. If this country ever does one day become a member of the Warsaw Pact or Comecon, it will surely be some English public school socialist who signs the treaty. And if that seems preposterous to those who think that Britain is different and can opt out of the consequences of making the state too mighty for its citizens, it at least highlights the thought that there is something worrying about a country where some of the more exotic flowers of its intellectual and social elite strive with such dedication to the destruction of the social order and the virtues of freedom and tolerance from which they have most benefitted. It may be that in some metaphorical sense it is true that each man kills the thing he loves, but well ordered societies take care to see that metaphor does not stray too prominently into the world of fact.

Russell Lewis
July 1978

1

WHO, WHOM?

Every political party has its rituals — the British Labour Party especially — and among those rituals there is none more colourful, evocative and symbolic than the Durham Miners' gala. For Labour's leader, no matter how pressing his other engagements, that one is a must. So it was that on the 18th July 1976 James Callaghan, who had recently become Prime Minister after Sir Harold Wilson's surprise resignation, found himself on Durham racecourse seated on a platform next to his predecessor as PM in the middle of 50 000 miners in carnival mood. They were both listening attentively to the speech of their colleague Michael Foot, Leader of the House, Callaghan's runner-up in the recent leadership contest, and the darling of the Left whose candidate he had been. Also seated there was Anthony Wedgwood Benn, now more often known at his own request as plain, no-nonsense, Tony Benn, who was Energy Secretary and therefore in effect supremo of Britain's newly gushing North Sea oil. He was much younger than his cabinet, or ex-cabinet, colleagues and looked it. Indeed, with his still slim and youthful figure and alert manner, he looked positively boyish against the background of their grey hairs. Yet there was about him then, as always, something which conveyed a slight feeling of unease to the onlooker. That could not be blamed on his pipe which gave him, if anything, a comfortable, old-fashioned, almost Baldwinesque appearance. It was perhaps, but not altogether, his general demeanour, jerky but intense. No, in the main it was his eyes, large and round beyond the ordinary and with a look so intense that, as James Fenton, the *New Statesman* political correspondent merrily remarked, it gave him an air of perpetual surprise.

Foot was in his element; this was his kind of audience. It always had been since in his youth, after leaving Oxford, while working for a shipping company in Liverpool, he had discovered the working classes and taken them to his heart. Indeed, he was so attached to them and to the unions — which alone in his eyes had the right to represent the workers — that once their interests were engaged there was no other group, demand, interest or principle which could get a look in. At the moment, however this *faux bonhomme* was at his most entertaining. He was talking about personalities, which, old pro that he was, he knew the crowds delight in. Now it was his colleagues' turn: 'There', he said, gesturing towards Wilson and Callaghan, 'the Prime Minister past and present', and then, turning towards Benn with a sweep of the arm, he added, 'the future.' According to James Wightman, the *Daily Telegraph* reporter on the spot, this drew a large cheer from the crowd. Mr Benn 'looked pleased,' Sir Harold 'nodded in agreement', but Mr Callaghan 'smiled wanly'.

The time soon came for Benn, the principal speaker, to say his piece, which he did with his accustomed panache, and with his demagogue's instinct for what his audience wanted to hear. He told the miners that the coal industry had a great future. Characteristically, he had the instant publicity quote: 'We have as many rigs looking for coal as for oil and gas. We have 300 years supply left', he said expansively.

We might be tempted to dismiss all this as a bit of festival frolic, with Foot performing his little harlequinade for the workers and seizing his chance to put in a plug for and repaying a debt to his fellow left-winger, who had withdrawn at an early stage from the recent leadership contest (since he knew he could not win but hoped to leave his 'marker' for the next time) and asked his supporters to vote for Foot. To be dismissive, however, would be a mistake. Like him or not, 'Wedgy', as he is known to his cronies, is a far from unlikely prospect as Labour leader — few members of parliament have in fact been more open about setting their sights on Number Ten. As he himself once said, he has never been interested in anything but politics, and he had the good fortune to arrive in the House of Commons at the age of twenty-five. Seniority, unappealing as it might be to one with so youthful an image, is one of his greatest advantages in a party currently led by a man who is of an age to bracket himself with Moses, and which — like the British armed forces — sets much store by getting some service in. Admittedly, Sir Harold Wilson, in terms of the historical comparisons in which he has lately and profitably been indulging on television, was very young as British Prime Ministers go; on the other hand he had spent many years in the House of Commons before he kissed the Queen's hand. Similarly, Benn has been in Parliament ever since he won Sir Stafford Cripp's old seat of Bristol South-East in 1950 — but for the brief interruption of that Commons career through involuntary transfer to the Lords (of which more anon), he would in due course be in the running for Father of the House.

Of course, simple longevity in a parliamentary party is not enough. Benn, however, has had a much longer career as a Minister than any of his contemporaries. He held two senior ministerial posts under Wilson's first two governments and two more senior posts since Labour's return to power in February 1974. He has been Chairman of the Fabian Society, has been for many years regularly elected to Labour's National Executive, and, even if in rather an eccentric fashion, chaired Labour's annual conference in 1972. Still more important he has a power-base on the left of the Labour party and though he has never actually been a

member of the Tribune group, he has willy-nilly, and almost
against their will, made himself the champion of the Left (of
which the Tribune group is the most explicit, articulate and
substantive expression). It is true that of late the whole
attempt of the Labour establishment under Callaghan has
been to avoid frightening the voters before the next general
election, and to that end the accepted idea is that the wild
men of the Left shall be put under wraps. But Benn has little
to worry about: time and trends within the Labour party are
conspiring on his side. The opposing Social Democratic wing
— even if occasionally (usually about the time of Labour's
annual conference) it springs to life in a Social Democratic
Alliance press release denouncing the influence of the
Commies and Trots — is practically finished as a real force in
the party. Its leaders have gone: above all, Roy Jenkins has
retreated to a comfortable and lucrative berth as President of
the European Commission in Brussels where he has been
joined — but not, as it turns out, for long — by David
Marquand, perhaps the most promising of the younger Social
Democrats; while Anthony Crosland, who taught Benn at
Oxford, has been lost through an untimely death. Another
young hopeful, the brilliant debater Brian Walden, has given
up his seat at Birmingham Ladywood to succeed Peter Jay,
the Prime Minister's accomplished son-in-law, in the lusher
pastures and, in a sense, larger constituency of a current
affairs programme broadcast at peak-time on Sunday.

Meanwhile, the dire straits of many social democrats in the
constituencies are too well-known to need much emphasis
here. It is sufficient to point to the sad case of Reginald
Prentice, whose constituency in Newham North-East was
taken over by certain militants who were said to favour Andy
Bevan. The latter is Labour's National Youth Officer and a
Trotskyist, whose appointment was detested and contested
by Callaghan and warmly defended by Benn ('Marxism has
from the earliest days been openly accepted by the party as
one of many sources of inspiration within the movement').
Prentice has since kicked over the traces and, like another

contemporary refugee from socialism, Mr Woodrow Wyatt, has declared himself a Conservative supporter. Yet for every individual like Prentice or Frank Tomney at Hammersmith North, who has been sacked for not towing the Marxist or Trotskyist line, how many have meekly succumbed and for the sake of their seat and their livelihood are now delegates of those leftist constituency executives, taking instruction on how to vote and which leaders to support?

Meanwhile, if the social democrats are weak, the left wing is strong. During the weak leadership of Harold Wilson, the classic trimmer of modern politics who surrendered to every pressure provided it was strong enough, the Left achieved dominance over the National Executive, supported by the trade unions who control two-thirds of the seats on that body and who supply the bulk of party funds. Nor has the left wing rested on its oars, but has used its dominance of the party machine to push through the 1976 Labour party conference a programme — from which incidentally the rules require that the next general election manifesto be drawn — which would take Britain further down the road to serfdom than the programme upon which the Italian Communist party stood at the last election. In 1977, however, Labour's conference was subdued, mindful as it was of the impending election. However the Marxist influence was still apparent, as the Social Democratic Alliance was quick to point out, from the fact that there were more fraternal delegates from the Soviet bloc than from the democratic socialist parties of the free world.

Material circumstance and the way the party dice are loaded thus seem to favour the eventual emergence of Tony Benn as Labour's leader, though it would be churlish to deny the extent to which he has by his own efforts made his own opportunities. Ever since Oxford, where he was a notable President of the Union and where he was already dedicated enough to spend an hour in preparation for every minute of his speech, he has been a formidable orator and debater. As with the Durham miners, so with more sophisticated

audiences, he has the flair for saying what is best calculated
to please his hearers. In debate he is invariably courteous and
agreeable to his opponents — a quality much appreciated in
the House of Commons. Above all, he has energy and single
mindedness: before he chopped his *Who's Who* entry in
1976, he had entered under the heading 'recreation' the
disarming 'staying at home with the family', and it seems that
outside politics that really is his only relaxation. He is a
tireless speaker and there is a story that during the October
1974 election he made four speeches in one day and then said
to his wife 'Let's make a night of it', by which he did not
mean, as any normal person would, going out to dinner, but
haring off to the workers' co-operative at Meriden at three
o'clock in the morning to look at their production line and
future plans. Benn is also abstemious to the point of
puritanism. He does not drink except for tea from a large
mug, though he does not seek to impose his teetotalism on
others, even though some have been irritated by his habit at
dinner in his own house of pointedly turning his glass upside-
down. He only smokes a pipe and, far from indulging in big
executive lunches, generally has sandwiches sent round to his
office in the Ministry.

Added to all this, his personal financial position is
unusually secure. Even if we ignore the Benn family money,
which is not negligible, Tony Benn's wife, Caroline (maiden
name Middleton de Camp) hails from a rich American
family. This fact alone must have relieved Benn from the
money worries afflicting many family men in public life,
which arise from the difficulty of reconciling the whole-
hearted pursuit of their political vocation with the proper
provision for the livelihood of their families and especially
the education of their children. He has had the great mental
comfort that — propose what radical and egalitarian policies
he may — he and his family would always have substantial
resources to fall back upon.

Bearing all these advantages in mind, what finally clinches
it as far as taking his prospects seriously is concerned, is

Benn's record of getting his own way — though whether that is mainly due to his will and determination or more because of his sure instinct in choosing those causes which are likely to win is a moot point. His most outstanding success was his campaign to be allowed to renounce his peerage and continue as an MP. He also had his way over stopping the creation of new hereditary peerages which have quietly lapsed, very likely for good since Mrs Thatcher shows no apparent intention of reviving them. Then the campaign to have a referendum to decide whether Britain should remain a member of the Common Market was one that Benn made all his own. And if the 1975 vote confirming membership was not to his taste, he had had his way against strong opposition to the actual principle of holding a referendum. Again he was able to push through, despite the doubts of his cabinet colleagues and the hostility of Whitehall, a series of schemes for workers' co-operatives which have wasted millions of pounds of tax payers' money. A more recent example of his ability to guide things his way was when he took up the cudgels on behalf of Andy Bevan, the Trotskyist Youth Officer of the Labour party, to ensure that his appointment to that post was confirmed. Although James Callaghan was fiercely opposed, Benn not only won but emerged personally unscathed and was allowed to carry on in his cabinet post as if nothing had happened.

It is because of this quality of survival and success that those who, like Bernard Levin, leading commentator of *The Times,* suggest that Benn is a lunatic whom nobody can take seriously should think again. His proven capacity to make an unpromising, even ridiculous, cause his own and to carry it through to victory however damaging the wider consequences, should give pause for thought. And Benn's moral earnestness — which some have identified as his boy scout syndrome — and his humourless and unrelenting do-gooding urges make him remarkably reminiscent of the tractarians of the last century and might make him unpopular with some, it does not necessarily make him ineffective.

Though he can be very persuasive, with industrial leaders, his real appeal is to the unsophisticated and is analogous to Jimmy Carter's electoral pitch to the Bible Belt in the USA. Puritanism is not necessarily the vote-loser that sceptical, clever, civilised people may think, for there is, and always presumably will be, a demand for the Billy Grahams of politics, with their simple certainties and their sure-fire promise of redemption, if only because in a time of decaying religion the sentiments which once sustained spiritual faith have been transplanted to the debased political sphere.

All these factors therefore make Benn a more than merely fanciful possibility as a future Labour leader, and subsequently, as Her Majesty's First Minister. This alone should be enough to justify a biography, since the provenance of a potential premier, his character, attitudes and opinions, the influences which have shaped him, his political friendships and alliances, and the group of people he is likely to bring with him to man the levers of power, must be of more than passing interest, especially to those who are likely to find him in control of their lives. That could have been the whole reason for undertaking this book, but it is not. It was not the promptings of a friendly curiosity or a benign pursuit of the real Benn which put pen to paper, but a more than ordinary mood of alarm at even the thought that one day he might hold the levers of prime ministerial power.

What justification can there be for such misgivings? In a democracy we must all reconcile ourselves to the idea that on occasion the other side will win. Is Benn such an extraordinary person after all? Is he not just another Philippe Egalité, an aristocrat who seeks to identify with the common people and like as not comes to a similarly sticky end? Unfortunately such people as Benn tend to involve other innocent folk in their eventual crash. But in addition, there is always something disturbing about people who are trying to de-classify themselves. Social climbers are bad enough, but what they are after is at least easily grasped. Social plungers, especially when their self-abasement appears to have an

ulterior motive, make one feel even more ill at ease. The
gradual proletarianisation of Benn, hilarious in one aspect,
looks sinister in another: can those who do not keep faith
with their roots remain faithful to anything else? It has been
mildly amusing to watch the Hon. Anthony Neil Wedgwood
Benn, after exerting himself so manfully to erase the title of
Lord Stansgate which he so unwillingly inherited, set about
ridding himself of the Anthony, the Neil and the Wedgwood
to emerge like a plucked chicken as plain Tony Benn. But is it
quite so diverting to see him rewrite his *Who's Who* entry
year by year and gradually eliminate all reference to his own
inherited privilege and social and cultural advantage? The
details are instructive. To take the entry under education as
an example: until 1969 this read 'Westminster School, New
College Oxford MA, 1949'; in 1970 the public school had
disappeared and so had New College — there was just the
laconic 'MA Oxford 1949'. It continued thus until 1972 when
it read 'MA Oxford 1949' and 'Since leaving university'.
However, the disadvantage of that was presumably that
reference remained to the fact that Benn had attended
university. So the following year it simply read 'Still in
progress'. Meanwhile the rest of the Benn entry, which had
remained full and unchanged right up until 1976, was
suddenly truncated from thirty-eight lines to the following:

> 'Benn, Rt Hon. Anthony Wedgwood, MP (Lab)
> Bristol South-East: Secretary of State for Energy.
> Address: House of Commons.'

In 1977 his entry disappeared completely from *Who's Who*.
     There is some risk no doubt in attaching too much
significance to trifles, but then again it is often in such small
things that the character of a man is writ large. For one
thing a man of genuine humility — and what else is the
insistence on the 'Tony Benn' about? — would scarcely care
what was entered under his name in *Who's Who* so long as it
was true. The gradual shrinking of what was entered under

the caption 'Education' to 'Since leaving University' and
finally to 'Still in progress' seems less an example of self-
effacement of the truly humble man, and more the conceit of
one who is anxious over every dot and comma. Doubtless
Benn's overall intention was to make himself more akin, and
therefore more acceptable, to the working class whose
political support he cherishes. Perhaps he romanticises
himself, feels converted, 'born again' like President Carter,
not like the latter in a religious sense, but as a worker whose
real education has been in the University of Life after leaving
Oxford. Just so, but it is Oxford which more than any other
institution, for better or worse, probably made him what he is
and which gave him a head start in political life, and it seems
a trifle ungrateful to set about deleting from the public record
the memory of the *alma mater* to which he owes so large a
debt. The same mentality was surely at work in the famous
Nationwide programme where Benn asserted that for two
years during the War he was an aircraftsman, second class,
and that later he became a salesman. Yet the record seems
clear from his own *Who's Who* entry before 1976: from 1943
to 1945 he was a Pilot Officer in the RAF and from 1945 to
1946 a Lieutenant in the Fleet Air Arm; nor did he mention
during the broadcast that his brief period as a salesman was
in the family business of Benn Brothers, the publishers.

How are we to interpret such attempts to alter history
retrospectively? Is there not something reminiscent of *1984,*
where the hero Winston had the daily task at the Ministry of
Truth of rewriting past leaders in *The Times*? The charitable
view is that it is vital for some creative and imaginative people
to think of themselves in some fanciful context; it mattered to
George Orwell to think of himself as a tramp, to Evelyn
Waugh to see himself as a decaying aristocrat, and to Frank
Harris to feel like a great lover — even though in each of
these cases the image was false. This sort of play-acting does
not much matter when indulged by writers and artists because
they do no-one else any harm, but a politician who goes in for
such Walter Mitty dreams has no such excuse for his

departure from reality. If it is a psychological necessity to Benn to cultivate a fantasy of an early manhood of social deprivation so that he can look back in synthetic anger, it must make one uneasy to think of him holding the top job in British politics.

However, if that were all we could wear it and him. British political history is full of devious people who have served the country well, from Halifax the Trimmer, to Walpole, to Lloyd George. The real worries must arise from the things Benn has done during his periods in office as a Minister, and from the radical ideas with which he has become identified. It is this record which most persuasively suggests that he cannot be trusted (to revive an old *Daily Mirror* expression) with his finger on the trigger. Added to the doubts aired above as to exactly how balanced he is, there is the certainty that when it comes to actual policies he is an extremist. And if the price of democracy, as we learn the hard way time and again, is eternal vigilance, that vigilance surely includes taking care that we do not put into positions of great power the kinds of extreme radicals who might shatter the delicately balanced politico-socio-economic structure which sustains our society. The details of Benn's career can be described chronologically in later chapters, but before going any further it is as well to summarise the policies and causes with which he has particularly identified himself and which justify taking him seriously as a threat to the freedom and prosperity of the British people.

What Benn has stood for most consistently is the concentration of ever more power in the hands of the government, especially a government which contains himself, and no-one has outdone him in enthusiasm for extending government control over the economy. He has been in the van of the movement for more nationalisation and indeed drew up the Labour party's nationalisation programme in 1974. That in itself might look like perfectly orthodox behaviour for a socialist minister, but Benn's constant harping on the idea that nationalisation is a means of root and branch change in our society has made his approach peculiarly sinister. As he put it at the Labour party conference in October 1971, 'We want industry to be in the public sector to change the power structure of our society'. These are not the words of a pragmatic politician but of one who sees politics as a crusade. Some might be attracted to such an attitude because it smacks of idealism, but experience shows that it is mostly idealists — those who want to fit their fellow men into some utopian mould or impose on them some blueprint of a perfect society — who become the most dictatorial. Those who are so sure of the righteousness of their ends are likely not to be too particular about the means they employ, or at any rate can view the pain and misfortune of others with equanimity, satisfied that it is all for the sake of a larger ultimate good.

Benn's approach has not been merely theoretical, since during his periods in office he has steadily, and with considerable success, endeavoured to extend the state's interventionist powers. As Minister of Technology from 1966 to 1970 he introduced the Industrial Expansion Act which was designed expressly to allow Ministers to move into the private sector through so-called schemes of industrial reorganisation. He himself used the Act's powers to effect the ill-fated merger between the Leyland Motor Company and British Motor Holdings to form British Leyland (which according to the latest wisdom should be broken up again). Again as Industry Minister after Labour regained power in 1974, he introduced the Industry Act which established the National Enterprise Board, giving himself added powers over private firms to make and enforce planning agreements and compulsory disclosure of company information. He then finished off British Leyland by nationalising it. Perhaps the urge for takeover was already compulsive: during his time as Minister of Industry, he later boasted, he nationalised sixty-two companies!

More than any other politician, Benn has been *the* campaigner for workers' control, and in a form which he insists should have nothing to do with the moderate type of scheme such as the co-determination found in West Germany — especially as the West German workers' approach is that of supporters of the capitalist social order. Instead he is explicitly drawn to the sort of direct action exemplified by workers taking over plants. Thus in October 1971 he applauded the work-in on the Upper Clyde and said, 'the workers in Upper Clyde Shipbuilding have done more in ten weeks to advance the cause of industrial democracy than all the blueprints we have worked on over the last ten years'. More generally, he has tried to formulate a doctrine of direct action (that is, workers taking the law into their own hands) as a form of democratic participation where the people force the rulers to act in accordance with their wishes in what he describes as 'fundamentally an educational exercise'. He was a moving spirit in the resoluton which was passed by the Labour conference in 1973 that the Clay Cross councillors who defied the law in the form of the Housing Finance Act should have any penalties retrospectively removed. Similarly, when Hugh Scanlon, the Engineers' Union leader, refused to recognise the Industrial Relations Act, Benn justified it on the grounds that 'conscientious objection to the law is not a criminal act' — hardly a self-evident truth because if it is, what does one say to the person (Bluebeard or Jack the Ripper?) who conscientiously objects to the law forbidding murder? Is it altogether fanciful to see here in the making a policy somewhat similar to the attempt (only just abortive) at direct industrial takeover by the supporters of Allende in Chile? Moreover, in support of any and everything that goes under the name of 'direct action', Benn, when in office, poured out millions of pounds of taxpayers' money in support of workers' co-operatives — at the Scottish Daily News, at Norton Villiers Triumph at Meriden, and at Kirkby Mechanical Engineering — though not one of them has proved viable.

His idea of workers' control has not only proved costly; it is likely to present a threat to freedom of expression. As an old BBC producer, he has long felt qualified to pronounce on all media matters. His most celebrated statement was to the Labour party conference in October 1972 when he exhorted all the workers in the media, especially for some reason the secretaries, printers and lift operators in Thomson House (home of *The Sunday Times*) to 'remember that they too are members of the working class movement and have a responsibility to see that what is said about us is true'. Earlier while he was still Minister of Technology, he had made a highly publicised attack on the BBC for not giving greater access to their programmes to strikers and protesting students and ended a diatribe against the Corporation with the ominous statement that 'broadcasting is too important to be left to the broadcasters'. This was generally interpreted as indicating his desire to eliminate the BBC's independence. It was therefore not surprising that when a Labour committee that he chaired produced a report on *The People and The Media* in July 1974, it suggested a scheme for replacing both the BBC and the IBA with an all-powerful politically-appointed Public Broadcasting Commission. This was paralleled by an equally Big Brotherish scheme for the press which suggested: a Communications Council to control the press; an Advertising Revenue Board to collect and allocate the advertising revenue of all publications; and preferential prices for newsprint for minority publications (a generous slice going no doubt to the *Morning Star* which has for years given Benn favourable publicity).

Yet another aspect of Benn's rather flesh-creeping theory of democracy is the idea that the Labour party conference, not the parliamentary Labour party, should formulate policy and elect the Leader. One has only to think how unrepresentative the Labour party conference is (especially because of union card votes) not merely of Labour voters, but even of paid-up Labour party members, to see the absurdity of this version of so-called grass-roots democracy. However, if absurd in principle, it would prove very convenient to Benn in practice because the party conference is dominated by the Left which regularly votes him and his radical friends to form a majority on the National Executive. Conference also happily supports extremist programmes such as those passed in October 1976. It is from 'the power base he has established in the NEC that Benn has dared a number of times to take issue with official cabinet policy. As chairman of the Labour party home affairs committee, he was responsible for the research department's producing in March 1975 — on the eve of Mr Healey's budget — its own draft budget, advocating more taxes on the self-employed, more state control and a surcharge on imports. In July of the following year the home affairs committee again campaigned against Healey's spending cuts. This committee has issued many more way-out documents, including one in March 1976 which sought to democratise the honours system (whether this included making Jack Jones a Companion of Honour did not at the time arise) and this gave Benn a launching pad from which to propose the abolition of the House of Lords. This, in a sense, completed the picture of the type of democracy Benn would like to give us: the Labour conference and the National Executive determining policy, with the Commons as a rubber stamp and not even with a feeble second chamber as at present to oppose the despotic power of any left-wing party with a transient majority.

If the above sketch of his ideas gives an impression that Benn is some sort of a socialist philosopher-king, a sort of Holland Park version of Marcuse or Sartre, that would foster a misunderstanding of the man: when Benn told the late Anthony Crosland (his old Oxford tutor) that he wanted to rid himself of the stigma of the intellectual, Crosland made the pointed reply that it was not possible to lose the stigma of the intellectual without first acquiring it. R.H.S. Crossman makes a similar comment more than once in his diary; for instance, on 22 October 1968 he mentions a conversation he had with Benn and Judith Hart, which ended with Benn giving them a copy of the speech he was due to deliver shortly afterwards. It was, says Crossman, 'an interminable

fourteen-page philosophical homily about participation. The
real trouble about Wedgy is that philosophically he is not
second-rate but non-existent. Curiously he has got this great
public relations sense, but he is not serious thinker.' Again,
commenting on Benn's much publicised speech on
democracy in May 1968, he said, 'The real problem with
Wedgy is that his presentation is brilliant, but what he says is
normally second-rate. This was one of the occasions when the
presentation was alpha and the content gamma minus.' At
yet another point Crossman referred to 'this inordinately
large Ministry of Industry headed by Wedgwood Benn, an
intellectually negligible whizz-kid, who simply cannot stand
up to Roy (Jenkins) at all'. Crossman was very shrewd and
perceptive about people and in this case he seems to have hit
the nail on the head. For Benn is significant not as an original
thinker, nor indeed as a thinker at all, but as a gifted
articulator of whatever thoughts happen to be fashionably
radical.

One has only to look at random at a set of press cuttings to
realise that it is Benn's publicity flair which is extraordinary.
Benn is indeed what he once called Crossman, 'a compulsive
communicator' — the medium in the Benn case being very
much the message, and the lack of any guiding principle
probably makes his utterances all the more frequent, fluent
and unrestrained. But, if he has himself no fully thought-out
political philosophy, he has become the voice of the Left
which seems at the moment poised to take over the Labour
party. This makes him important not in himself, but as the
channel of radical political trends and forces in today's
Britain. He even on one occasion admitted as much 'There is
a wind of change blowing through British industry ... I am no
more than a weather cock showing which way it is blowing.'

It is in this sense of epitomising certain significant
tendencies of our time that makes Benn the guru of
corporatism, the made-to-order bionic man of British
socialism, who, if he did not exist, would have to be invented.
So the most convincing picture of Benn is not of the

prospective puppet master, more of one who is a puppet himself, manipulated by certain blind, primitive and venal forces like envy and union boss ambition. He seems almost Pinocchio-like in his innocence, innocence not of personal ambition certainly, but of envy — in the material sense why should he envy anyone since he is to an extent insulated from the worst excesses of the plundering tax man? And he gives the impression of a lack of malevolence surprising in a man of the Left, an impression strengthened by his elaborate courtesy to opponents in debate. He is for all the world like a sorcerer's apprentice, but without as yet any sense of horror about the malignant elements which he has stirred up. There we see him, in shirt-sleeve order, collar undone, pipe thrust out aggressively, arms gesticulating jerkily, his saucer-like blue eyes revolving with excitement and delight and a kind of insane optimism, while from his lips pours forth a stream of newspeak about the techno-servo-socio-economico-participatory electronic feedback to the computerised super atomic laser-bright regeneration of Britain. It is because of his slightly robotic behaviour that Benn strikes many observers as slightly comic, but ridicule is inappropriate. In a way it is more serious if he is unconsciously responding to voices in the air, always anxious to be the first to expound the idea whose time has come, than if he were a genuine prophet. Swept on by his uncomprehending enthusiasm for all that is radical and new, he has little idea of where all this frantic neophilia is taking him or those whose futures he has power to decide. Edmund Burke understood well enough the danger of such people as Benn when he wrote, 'The passion for innovation is the character of small minds', and perceived that this was the kind of mentality which led in the end to the excesses of the French Revolution. If we are to avoid similar extremes, we should take heed of the peril now: in Benn, because he is the sort of person he is, we are able to see gift-wrapped in one personality and in an exaggerated form most of the urges which are conspiring to make Britain a corporate state, full of the trappings of democracy but nearer in essence to the Star Chamber style of government than anything we have seen since Stuart times.

Nor is this alarming figure of Benn as a kind of personification of our woes to be dismissed as a biographer's fancy formulation or as a spuriously neat parcelling up of the subject in an attempt to impose an artificial unity on a life where there is only the play of the contingent. Indeed, not for nothing have the twenty-eight turbulent years of Benn's parliamentary career coincided with Britain's protracted decay, and the study of the ceaseless flow of Benn's utterances during those years, as of the political actions and campaigns associated with those utterances, strongly suggests an organic connection between that decline and the ideas to which he is unerringly drawn.

Though inclined, as we have seen, to deny, even so far as it lay in his power to expunge, those portions of his past which are embarrassing or politically inconvenient, he has willy-nilly come to identify himself with — indeed become — the very embodiment of those trends and policies, the furtherance of which can only send his country into even more headlong decline and speed it even faster along the road to serfdom. They include the drift towards magnified state regulation and control, the sustained attempt to impose greater economic equality, especially through mounting and ever more 'progressive' taxation with the consequent and disastrous erosion of incentives. In addition there is the strengthening of an already dangerously extended trades union power, the encouragement of militancy and direct action on the shop floor, the fostering of the extremist, leftist, often Trotskyist, groups in their increasingly successful attempts to take over the Labour party from within, plus the tendency quite deliberately to erode the natural bases of a pluralist democratic society and to remove the institutions which pluralism naturally supports like the House of Lords and an independent BBC. They include finally the adoption of a non-cooperative attitude towards our European community partners and the rest of the world too, shown in the sponsorship of barren beggar-my-neighbour economic policies in the attempt, eventually self-defeating, to placate certain domestic interest groups, especially unions anxious to recreate jobs destroyed by excessive wage settlements. For all these tendencies, which in the long or even the medium run can spell isolation and ruin for the British economy and polity, Benn provides much of the immediate inspiration and all too often the most strident voice.

Of course, in human affairs nothing is inevitable, and by timely action there are evils — especially those of politicians' contriving — which we may avoid. That is why it is vital to locate what the threats are, and whence they come. The value of Benn from this point of view is that he is a natural focus for the most lethal collectivist ideas of our epoch. The account in this chapter of Benn's activities is not exhaustive but merely representative, and the ensuing pages will show that they are consistent with the rest of his behaviour. It is not too much to say that, in analysing Benn's career opinions and actions, we are confronting a miniaturised compendium of the errors which have come to be called the 'British disease'. Thus it is that while some biographies are eulogies, some cautionary tales, this book is nothing if not a warning.

2

FROM WEDGWOOD BENN TO LORD STANSGATE ...AND BACK

1925~64

The first the British public heard of the Hon. Anthony Neil Wedgwood Benn, was in 1946 after he returned to Oxford after the War. It was of course natural that as the son of a Labour peer he should be an undergraduate at New College — the recognised mecca of Labour's governing elite. He did not however conform to the usual pattern of attending Winchester, being a product of another old public school connected with a cathedral, Westminster. Even there his schoolmates had already got the message that Wedgy was destined for a political career, and for that Oxford was the ideal apprenticeship. Success in the Union had long been the stepping-stone to political advancement, curiously enough to a far greater extent than Cambridge which had a Union equally distinguished but which has never produced a single Prime Minister, whereas at Oxford their name is legion.

Gladstone, for instance, had proceeded almost by osmosis from the front bench at the Oxford Union to the government front bench in the House of Commons. It was to Benn's great credit that in the Union of post-war Oxford he shone more brightly than any; it was a period of unusual talent when several generations of undergraduates, whose education had been postponed by war, were compressed into a few years. These were not callow youths but veterans of many a campaign, men who were mature, who had lived and in many cases stared death in the face, and at an early age had taken on frightening responsibilities. Among these Benn was the star. He was by all accounts one of the finest presidents the Oxford Union had ever had. It was said of the young Macaulay that he arrived at Cambridge with his amazing oratorical style already completely formed, and there was something of the same quality about Benn. He was unusually articulate, polished and always ready to deal with the interrupter with a witty retort, but without animus. He was almost as much of a hero with the Conservatives as with the Socialists, perhaps partly because he looked the part of a young Tory radical, almost a reincarnation of Lord John Manners, Disraeli's young friend. Like Manners, Benn was the epitome of Young England with his fair hair, good looks, slim build and jaunty aristocratic self-confidence — which was just as well, because the tone of the university was decidedly Tory as shown by the voting in Union debates. If Benn *was* radical, he was not very noticeably so. Indeed, according to Union President Nicholas O'Shaughnessy, speaking in March 1978, the old pre-tin mug, pre-proletarian Benn was still fondly remembered by Scouts (college servants) at New College: 'Benn used to insist on his title, the Hon. Anthony Wedgwood Benn being used outside his room'. O'Shaughnessy recalled, 'He also liked to be addressed by his full RAF rank. Of course his politics were very different too.' Benn's list of debating motions when he was President was very conventional, the only one which might in retrospect seem to betray his more radical future intentions was the motion (for which he spoke himself) that 'The house deplores the present state of the British Press', which he won though on a small total vote.

Given Benn's talents, it was only natural that when the Institute of International Education fixed up a five-month debating tour for Oxford speakers to visit forty-three states in America, he should be the leader. The other two were Sir Edward Boyle, later to hold several Ministerial posts in Conservative governments and to retire early to a peerage and the post of Vice-Chancellor at Leeds, and Kenneth Harris of subsequent television fame. Harris's book about that trip *Travelling Tongues* still retains a freshness and charm and aptly conveys the terrific impact in America of what was surely the most famous and successful of all the old university Union debating visits there. The trio quite rightly returned like conquering heroes. Harris's witticism in the debate they all attended on their return is still remembered. He said 'I had a terrible time. I was the only commoner on the trip (Benn was an Hon. and Boyle was a baronet). I even had to clean their shoes.'

Where had this extraordinary Charles James Fox-like figure sprung from? Benn is the product of a long line of radical non-conformists, which reached back to at least his great-grandfather, the Reverend Julius Benn, who was once sacked from his job as headmaster for marching all his pupils out of an Anglican church in the middle of a sermon during which the vicar attacked Martin Luther. According to cousins, the 'Wedgwood' which first appeared in Anthony's father's name, stems from an incident in the early life of John Williams Benn who had run away from home and was befriended by a member of the Wedgwood family in Liverpool who also gave him his start in life. John Benn, Anthony's grandfather, lived in Stepney and later became a Liberal MP and chairman of the London County Council. Anthony's father, William Wedgwood, went to London University and gained a first in French. He began the publishing firm of Benn Brothers with his brother Ernest.

Both brothers became Liberal MPs, Ernest becoming an arch Liberal individualist, while William Wedgwood Benn moved leftwards. The latter served in the Great War with great distinction in the Royal Flying Corps, winning the DFC. The war over, he returned to politics and after some years joined the ranks of the Labour party; thus he unusually became more left-wing as he grew older, in this respect setting an example which his son has followed. He became Secretary of State for India in Ramsay Macdonald's ill-fated last Labour government and when Gandhi came to London for talks, he was introduced to young Anthony, one of the latter's first political recollections. When the National Government was formed William Benn resigned, but he was back in the House in 1937 after a by-election, and like his son later, topped the poll for the Labour Shadow Cabinet in 1939. All the same, he decided to join the forces in 1940, despite his age of sixty-three years. In 1941 he was made a peer to increase Labour's representation in the House of Lords. He consulted his eldest son, Michael, who had no political ambitions and consequently no objections. He naturally enough did not ask Anthony who was only sixteen at the time, though apparently he was furious, as it turned out with reason since Michael, who as a fighter pilot had like his father won the DFC, was killed, making Anthony heir to the title.

There is no doubt that Anthony Wedgwood Benn was greatly influenced by his father, both politically in his radicalism (over such causes as women's rights) and in other things like his meticulous filing system and squirrel-like obsession with collecting data and classifying it. An Oxford contemporary recalls a visit to the family (including younger brother David, also at Oxford and then to the left of Anthony) and found them very good fun. They all talked at once, except when father spoke, when they all fell respectfully silent: he was a great raconteur.

At Oxford Benn met a research student studying seventeenth century literature, a pretty girl called Caroine Middleton de Camp, who came from a very well-to-do

American family from Cincinnati, Ohio. After a whirlwind
courtship lasting a week, he proposed and she accepted. He
has since acquired the park bench on which he popped the
question from Oxford City Council and it is now placed in
front of their home in Holland Park. They started as they
were fated to go on and spent their honeymoon at a political
summer school. This was an unusually happy marriage,
blessed in due course with three sons and one daughter.
Caroline was remembered by one Oxford contemporary as a
supporter of Wallace, the far left Democratic candidate for
the US Presidency and apparently she was far more radical in
her views than Benn at this time. She is generally given a lot
of the credit — if that is the word — for the leftward drift of
his subsequent political career. Her own interests were mainly
in education and she became later an ardent campaigner for
comprehensive schooling.

After leaving Oxford Benn first briefly worked in the
family firm of Benn Brothers as a salesman and then became
a producer on the North American service of the BBC. His
political chance came when Sir Stafford Cripps's seat in
Bristol South-East fell vacant in 1950. The Reverend Mervyn
Stockwood (the present Bishop of Southwark), who was on
the local committee choosing the candidate for Labour,
talked to Tony Crosland, who had been Benn's tutor at New
College and who strongly recommended his pupil. Benn made
an excellent speech and won the nomination. Thus,
although since boyhood he had always thought in terms of a
parliamentary career, he was a little surprised to find himself
— deservedly no doubt but also partly as a result of the old
boy network — a candidate for a safe parliamentary seat.

At the time of the by-election in November 1950 the
Labour government was struggling, with a small
parliamentary majority and its popularity in the country was
at a low ebb: prices were rising in the shops; food was
rationed and the rations were small; housing was short;
defence costs were rocketing. In the campaign therefore Benn
was inevitably on the defensive, for instance blaming the

rising cost of living on world conditions over which the
Government had no control. Yet the visionary was even now
in evidence and already there was in embryo his later
obsession with worker democracy; so he spoke generally
about Labour's plans to mould society on new lines and how
the big obstacle to their fulfilment was the maldistribution of
wealth, which placed economic power in the hands of a few
people. Nationalisation was the cure, he felt. Yet he also had
critical words to say about one nationalised industry, the
BBC — where he had just been working and therefore had to
keep his comments muted — which he castigated as
'exceedingly backward in the field of consultation. My own
union, the National Union of Journalists, is not even
recognised by the BBC.' Jennie Lee (wife of Nye Bevan, then
Minister for Health) came and spoke for him and so did
another MP, Ian Mikardo, then a bright young hope of the
Left. However, despite such help, Benn could not have
expected a marvellous result when the tide was running
against Labour, and was perhaps relieved that, although his
majority was down by half, it was still over 7000 and he was
safely elected, notching the Government's overall majority in
the Commons up from four to five. What was more, at
twenty-five he was the youngest English member of the
Commons. He was photographed as the new Member
shaking hands with a blasé policeman. The next day the
policeman failed to recognise him and shooed him away from
the House. He was soon nicely settled in though, and he and
Caroline found a flat at Chiswick right next to the
underground to Westminster.

In those early days in the Commons, even if he already had
hankerings after radical ideas, Benn was a pretty
conventional kind of Labour MP, with conventional enough
views, condemning for example the Conservatives'
'imperialism', and arguing at a divisional garden party in
Bristol held in the summer of 1951 at the time of the Iran oil
dispute — the Iranians had taken a leaf out of the British
Labour party's book and nationalised the assets of what is

now British Petroleum — that Britain's influence in the world rested not upon her battleships, but on 'what our leaders are saying in the world and the success we are having in meeting our own domestic problems'.

In October 1951 there was a general election and the Tories under Winston Churchill were returned. With nothing to hope for from office, Benn's natural drift towards radical courses could now proceed without inhibition. He was drawn into the peace lobby and was enthusiastically written up in *Peace News* for the unoriginal pronouncement in a speech to a Bristol conference: 'Peace is the most important problem of the present time'. Yet his drift leftwards was slow enough; in the summer recess of 1952 he went for a long visit to the United States and missed the Labour conference, but as a result he was, he said, 'very friendly with everybody' on his return to the House. In other words, he was not caught up in the controversy over the Bevanites. He went to their meetings, but deplored personal attacks and called for a united party. 'No one is bigger than the party', he said on his return on 19 October, trying to take on the role of peacemaker between the rival factions.

In February 1954, Benn was involved in an interesting clash with what was later to be called the 'Establishment' over nineteen-year-old Paul Garland, a Queen's Scout from Bristol, who was also a Communist — indeed, he was District Secretary of the West of England Young Communist's League. Garland was billed to broadcast on the West Regional Home Programme, but this was cancelled after complaints by a number of local Conservative MPs and he was subsequently disowned by the Boy Scouts Association. Benn, apparently outraged at this limitation of free speech, challenged the Chief Scout, Lord Rowallan, to debate the case in public, but his lordship — perhaps wisely—refused.

A big step in the development of Benn, the radical, was his early entry into the campaign against the hydrogen bomb. He was one of the small bunch of Labour MPs — the leading spirit among whom was that long-established pacifist, Fenner

Brockway — who formed part of a thirty-strong poster parade at Westminster at the end of April 1954. They were passing the Ministry of Housing and Local Government when the Minister, Harold Macmillan, came down the steps, shook Brockway's hand and said, 'I'm glad to see you true to your cause'. Fenner Brockway was an old friend of Benn's father (who, on being appointed Secretary of State for India under Ramsay Macdonald's last Labour administration, had almost immediately called Brockway and Jimmie Maxton in to advise him). This demonstration was the beginning of the movement which led to the CND and the Aldermaston marches of which Benn was an enthusiastic supporter.

Brockway also brought young Benn into another of his activities, namely the Movement for Colonial Freedom (MCF) for which Benn chaired the Committee on South-East Asia. The MCF also sponsored broader organisations such as the Anti-Apartheid Movement, the British Council for Peace in Vietnam and the Chile Solidarity Committee. The MCF, though it included Harold Wilson among the sponsors and had Anthony Greenwood as treasurer, got into some trouble with the rather rightist Labour party of the time because it had members, including Communists, who were members of proscribed organisations. Probably because of the presence of Brockway, who was a genuine old-style Labour idealist, the MCF was not itself proscribed, but involvement with these groups brought Benn into a far more left-wing milieu than he would naturally have been drawn into had Labour been in power; then he would almost certainly have been brought early into the ruling establishment. It was Benn's energy and the comparative lack of constructive outlets for it during the long period of opposition with which his life as an MP began which exposed him to radical influences that in other circumstances might have passed him by.

It was not strange for Benn, as an influential MCF figure, to take a leading part in the big demonstration held in Trafalgar Square when the Suez Crisis broke. On 16 September 1956 he addressed a crowd of 7000 people asking

why, if Colonel Nasser had done something wrong, did not
Britain take the case to the International Court? The reason,
he suggested, was that Anthony Eden merely wanted to
impose his will on Nasser, whose real crimes in Eden's eyes
were 'ridding Egypt of the monarchy and dreaming about an
Empire'. 'I am afraid', he went on, 'to sit opposite 300 MPs
who dream of an empire all their lives.' He jeered at the
sudden way the Tories had developed an affection for
internationalisation. Amidst laughter he asked, 'Is there any
Conservative in the House of Commons who would support
the internationalisation of the oil industry?' In a sense one
might have said that the industry was internationalised
already, though in private hands — the multinational bogeys
of Labour propaganda of later years — but it was a shrewd
point all the same, and effectively mocked the unholy mess
into which Eden had plunged the Tories in his abortive
attempt to solve the Middle Eastern problem by resort to
arms, without ensuring first that the Americans would wear
it.

One result of the Anglo-French intervention in Egypt was
that it diverted world attention from Hungary where the
Soviet tanks rolled in to crush an attempt to introduce
personal freedoms of speech, opinion and elections of the
western type into a communist society. Benn, together with
four other MPs — Fenner Brockway, Richard Crossman,
Barbara Castle and George Wigg — who claimed that they
had always worked for a closer understanding with the
Soviet Union, wrote to complain indignantly to *Pravda,* the
official newspaper of the Communist Party of the USSR,
asking whether its description of the Hungarian rising as
'counter-revolutionary' would apply to 'any system of
government which permitted political parties opposed to
Communism'. *Pravda* published the letter and predictably
asserted that the aim of the uprising was to establish a Fascist
regime. Perhaps after this incident the five MPs were
themselves at last starting to achieve a genuinely closer
understanding of what the Soviet Union was like.

Soviet policy towards Hungary may have had a disillusioning effect on Richard Crossman, who was at this stage making no secret of his loss of sympathy for the doctrinaire left-wing socialists of whose group he was so long a leading member. As a result, Crossman found his vote slumping heavily the constituency section in the Labour conference ballot for the National Executive. Benn, on the other hand was just behind Sidney Silverman at the head of the list of those not elected. This surely indicated that Benn had now made the grade as a figure of some consequence in the Labour party. He had from the first shown a talent as a speaker for putting even jejune ideas in a compelling, provocative and often interestingly off-beat way. This was already apparent in his maiden speech in the House of Commons on 7 February 1951, when, in referring to the iron and steel industry, he said that it would be 'psychologically disastrous' at a time when there was a real threat to the country's standard of living to have an iron and steel industry 'which was doing very well from a business point of view'. This statement had about it that slightly perverse quality which attracts attention and is apt to make headlines.

Benn's improved standing on the Labour party secured his election for the first time to the National Executive, narrowly defeating Ian Mikardo, who after more years on the Executive was thus prevented from taking the Chair. The general election of 1959 had been lost, but Benn had been anchorman for Labour's thirteen election television and radio broadcasts, and most people considered that he had done a very good professional job. ('This is not a television election', he had said, subtly disowning any attempt to influence the viewer in the opening programme. Insofar as it *was* a television election it was no fault of Benn's that the bravura performance was by Harold Macmillan — 'You never had it so good' was something which Labour could not match.) Gaitskell subsequently showed his gratitude for Benn's work in the election by making him spokesman on Transport in his Shadow Cabinet.

Following his appointment, Benn, with his customary energy, almost immediately introduced in December 1959 a private member's bill for the better control of traffic. Like many other private member's bills, it did not go through to the third reading, but it dealt with a highly topical issue — congestion — and when in the following April the Minister, Ernest Marples, came to put forward a bill for the Government, he was not afraid to borrow Benn's main proposal that the Minister should be given a much freer hand to control traffic. Benn continued very effectively to badger Marples on this topic, asking him to learn from the tidal flow techniques of the Americans and from their tougher ways with drunken drivers. Before the Whitsun holiday, he was insisting that a proper control would stem the slaughter on the roads which was too complacently accepted by the Ministry as due to the 'human factor' over which it had no power. In all this, Benn was reflecting the conventional wisdom of the time which was for many years to turn every national holiday into a misery fest with the Minister regularly scolding drivers for their disgraceful driving. In reality however, though regulation and control had their place, the holiday accidents were not vastly different from those at other times of the year and where variations did occur, they reflected such mundane factors as the volume of traffic and the weather. The regular bank holiday moral lecture by the Transport Minister has now happily ceased.

At this time Benn also further enhanced his standing with the Left of the party by forming his Algeria Committee to encourage a negotiated peace for that country, a bit of gratuitous interference which caused considerable annoyance in France.

At the end of the 1950s it was becoming increasingly likely that Benn, despite his dislike for the House of Lords — in a Fabian pamphlet in January 1957 he had put forward his pet scheme for making the Privy Council into a second chamber to replace the House of Lords — would soon succeed his aged father to the peerage. In December 1954 Benn had sent a petition to the House of Lords for permission to renounce the title, but in February the request had been turned down by a committee of six peers. After this no-one really believed that when his father died Benn could avoid being pushed up into the Lords. Indeed, after a highly competent performance in the Commons when speaking on the Air estimates in June 1957 he had been tipped by *Reynolds News* to become Labour's leader in the Lords. In 1960 that fate might even have seemed attractive since the smooth tenor of his political career was interrupted by a serious miscalculation.

It was in the run-up to the party conference that Benn made his great mistake, seeing himself rather grandiosely as peacemaker between the nuclear disarmers who wanted Britain to abandon the bomb unilaterally and the official leadership which thought that the bomb should be kept as long as the Russians had it. Frank Cousins put forward a resolution at the Labour's 1960 annual conference held at Scarborough, calling for a unilateral banning of the bomb. Benn sailed in, calling for party unity, urging that the official resolution and the Cousins resolution were quite compatible. In effect, he was arguing that the conference should face both ways and that a logical nonsense was less disastrous than a party split. He was not alone because George Brown, the Shadow Defence spokesman, was also in favour of the facing-both-ways approach, and urged that the conference should support both resolutions. The Executive would have none of Benn's suggestion that Cousins should come and discuss areas of agreement between the two resolutions. At this Benn angrily stormed out, resigning from the Executive in protest against the way the union leaders had laughed off his efforts as peacemaker. He had in fact been a bit too clever. He had argued that there was no basic difference between the two resolutions, so honest men could vote for both. He had also argued that if Frank Cousin's resolution was carried the split would be so serious as to wreck the party. In any case, though it gave Benn much publicity, it did not win him gratitude from either side. Nor did it enhance his reputation with the conference which was shown when the elections came to the Executive and he lost his place to Ian Mikardo, an outright unilateralist.

At this point Benn quit the Gaitskell camp, saying that he could not support as candidate for party leader one who pledged to fight, fight and fight again against conference decisions, and threw in his lot with Harold Wilson. Benn's prospects at this juncture must have appeared very uncertain even to himself. He had abandoned one leader, whom he found too dogmatic and inflexible, and transferred to another, who was as flexible and resilient as a rubber band. Moreover, Wilson was not Labour's favourite at this time, not among the parliamentary Labour party anyway, and fell from first to ninth place in the Shadow Cabinet elections. At this point fate took a hand and what looked like the end of Benn's political career was converted into a means of making, or at least opening up, his way to the top. For in November 1960 his father, Lord Stansgate, died and the title passed to Benn. He had already fought harder than most men to keep out of the House of Lords than most do to enter. In any event, he decided to fight again and this proved perhaps the most important single episode in his career, because it made him a public figure, because it strengthened his already radical tendencies and dislike of the established order (of which the House of Peers was, to him personally, the oppressive symbol) and because it developed his taste for the populism which was so strong an ingredient in this early success.

The campaign began without delay. Benn announced his intention of not accepting his elevation and tried all means to avoid going 'upstairs', dramatically returning the letters patent of his title to the Lord Chamberlain at Buckingham Palace and formally executing an instrument of renunciation of the Stansgate peerage. He perhaps already sensed, with that instinct for the new trend which is one of his most useful gifts, that the whole climate of opinion had changed. Later on the myth grew up that Benn had fought alone against the odds and against the Establishment to remain a commoner but, without in the least disputing or denigrating Benn's own considerable exertions, the fact was that most people — and, strange to relate, most of the Establishment — were on his side. It was not only his old friend the Bishop of Southwark; it was not only young Tory Peers, or prospective peers like Lord Altrincham and Lord Lambton, MP who might be suspected of wanting to do some renouncing on their own behalf; nor was it just lefty Conservative MPs like Humphry Berkley. It included the greatest living Conservative (or for that matter Englishman) Winston Churchill, and that arch-establishment figure, Lord Salisbury. There were Conservative journalists like Malcolm Muggeridge and T.E. Utley. The Oxford University Conservatives passed a resolution in his favour and Sir Gerald Nabarro sent his campaign fund £25.00.

In his campaign Benn did not miss a trick. He went through the usual channels, that is through the Committee of Privileges of the House, and was turned down in March 1961. The Tory government rather unwisely would not let him make his plea from the bar of the House the following month, and this was angrily contested by many backbench Tory MPs. So he released to the press the speech that he would have given. He then proceeded, with the full support of his constituency Labour party, to stand in the ensuing by-election, the Liberals obligingly refusing to put up a candidate. He pledged himself dramatically to fight even if it meant facing jail or bankruptcy — and indeed he could have faced a fine of £500 a day for sitting as an MP while disqualified. His Tory opponent, Malcolm St. Clair, was oddly enough another heir to a peerage. Benn fought his campaign with gusto and must have been highly encouraged that the Prime Minister, Harold Macmillan (largely it was said to defuse the issue) set up a committee to propose measures of Lords reform. In any event, he won by a thumping majority of over 13 000 votes — double what it had been at the last general election.

Still stealing the show, Benn shortly afterwards got himself
dropped from the *Tonight* programme because they would
not call him 'MP'. Even more dramatically, on 8 May, he
was barred from entering the House of Commons by a
doorkeeper, a dignified figure who had once been a
Sergeant-Major, and later when the question was raised in
the House, R.A. Butler, speaking for the Government, was
shouted down. Malcolm St. Clair went to the High Court and
lodged a petition to invalidate Benn's election, but to add to
the fun of the thing, the same day the official record, the
London Gazette, declared that Benn was elected. So there
was a court case and all in a blaze of publicity of which Benn
took the maximum advantage, appearing in court with
ninety-one law books, with the aid of which he argued
eloquently and continuously for five days, that is to say for
twenty-two hours. In showbiz terms it was unbeatable, but
he lost his case. He had a bill of £8000 and Malcolm St. Clair
was declared elected. St. Clair now offered to resign if Benn
would promise not to stand again unless he was qualified to
do so, but Benn, in rather ungracious fashion, refused.

He was now a highly popular figure in the Labour party. In
November he headed the Fabian poll. In February 1962 he
was called upon to address the Durham Miners' Gala, a
singular honour since he was the first peer to do so for ninety-
one years, and at the party conference in October he was
elected back on to the National Executive, this time ousting
Jim Callaghan. He was loudly applauded at the conference
when he welcomed the Executive's anti-Common Market
statement and declared that there would be an election on the
issue. During all this time he had not been idle politically
either, but had been especially prominent in protests about
foreign affairs over the Portuguese oppression in Angola and
Goa, American bullying of Cuba, and (with all his family
joining in a protest march) over the South African bloodshed
at Sharpeville. His wife, Caroline, had also been busy and
had published a novel *Lion in a Den of Daniels,* surely
autobiographical, about an American girl's reactions to

Britain which she found 'decadent', though this she said patronisingly was not knocking Britain because both she and her husband thought decadent countries were 'nice'.

All this was the prelude to the real triumph in December 1962, when a joint committee of both Houses of Parliament recommended in favour of Benn's cause. He immediately announced that he would be outside the Chancellor's rooms with a camp bed and a flask as soon as the law was passed so as to make his application without delay. At the end of May 1963 the Bill which was to allow him to disown his title was published, in July it was passed and at the end of the month the newspapers were again alive with accounts of Benn — this time holding a celebration tea party for his supporters in the House of Commons. In the meantime he had already been re-adopted by Labour for Bristol South-East. It was some indication of a more general recognition that at this point he was also made head of the new Fabian International Bureau in early August. A fortnight later, title duly renounced, he opened his by-election campaign, which he concluded victoriously with a bumper majority of 15 479 over his opponent Edward Martell. At the Labour conference he was naturally treated as a hero and to cap it all he came third in the poll for the party's National Executive.

Benn had energetically pursued his own cause and had had his reward. In the process, in a rather unexpected way, he had made history, and, aided by chance, had set in train events which were to transform the political situation on the other side of the fence as well. At the Tory conference delegates received the news that Harold Macmillan, their leader and Prime Minister, had been struck down by illness and that a new leader would have to be found. It quickly became apparent at that conference that the most popular man there was Lord Home. Of course, ever since Baldwin had pipped Curzon at the post, it had been clear that no peer could ever become Prime Minister, and therefore Leader, again. Yet Benn had removed that fatal obstacle and it fell to Home to form a new Conservative government. The latter's inexperience matched against Wilson's accomplished parliamentary technique proved fatal to the Tories' recovery, and Benn, just appointed Commonwealth spokesman for Labour, must have realised that the prize of office was just within his grasp.

3

POSTMASTER GENERAL VERSUS THE PEOPLE

1964~6

The 1964 general election was delayed until the last minute because Sir Alec Douglas-Home, the Conservative Prime Minister (in his youth an ardent cricketer and later President of the MCC) needed time to play himself in. This had the effect of making the year or so beforehand a period of continuous electioneering, during which Harold Wilson, powerfully aided by Benn on the broadcasting side of the exercise, managed to put over very effectively both the negative message about the thirteen wasted years of Tory rule and the positive and beguiling promise of white-hot-technological revolution in which Labour's new Britain would be forged.

For Benn in his constituency it was something of a re-run of the election he had already fought just over a year before, though no two elections are ever quite the same. It was enlivened however by an unusual if trifling incident. Unknown to the victim, he took a tape recording of a journalist from the *Western Daily Press,* Paul Fluck, with whom he conducted a rather heated interview. The conversation was about an article Fluck had written criticising Harold Wilson for not replying to a telegram, allegedly sent on behalf of 28 500 Bristol parents, about the snub Wilson was supposed to have administered them over the comprehensive school plan. Benn got hot under the collar about misrepresentation of the facts and reported the paper to the Press Council. Mr Fluck, unused to all this apparatus of the technological revolution — it was some time before Watergate — reported the fact Benn had recorded him without first seeking permission to the National Union of Journalists — a fair *quid pro quo.*

The election campaign showed Benn in his element with the new gadgetry — his office in Holland Park Road was like a campaign Ops room, lined with filing boxes and charts. One chart was a super campaign diary with coloured hieroglyphics, showing his own and Harold Wilson's movements, dates of the Bristol campaign and of television appearances. He was the anchor man of Labour's election broadcasts and was very effective in the role, especially at the negative job of knocking the Tories for their incompetence — their stop-go and bad planning — and their lack of concern for the ordinary person — the Rent Act and the Beeching Rail closures being prize exhibits.

All too soon the election was over and Labour, if only by a whisker, had won. To the victors the spoils of office, and in the new appointments the still youthful Benn was made Postmaster General. It is possible that the appointment owed something to the article which Benn had written on the Post Office in the *Guardian* in June 1964. He argued that this, the oldest of the nationalised industries, was where the great breakthrough into developing science-based industries as key points of growth in the economy would come — a theme which could hardly have been improved upon by old White

Heat (of the technological revolution) Wilson himself. Some rejoiced at the thought that this young, dynamic Minister would put new life into a Victorian institution; others, who reflected that he was now in charge of broadcasting and that he was no friend of the independent companies, were alarmed. Both reactions were, perhaps, over-political. For being Postmaster General was above all else an organisational job and in that sense perhaps an anachronism (arising from the fact that the Post Office had been a nationalised industry time out of mind). That was why it was still run by a Minister, with the snag that it was therefore a football in the parliamentary arena where the details of its operation could be kicked around. Even so, running the Post Office was a big business operation, with a staff of 400 000. Also, mainly because of the exploding demand for telephones (and therefore for telephone exchanges, cables and vehicles) it was a huge capital spender. That was why Ernest Marples — a man almost bereft of political ideas, but possessing an amazing capacity for getting things done as long as he was pointed in the right direction — had been such a success as PMG.

The story is told that on the morning of his arrival at his new Ministry, Benn was brought tea in a most elegant silver service. This he dismissed and demanded to have it in his usual proletarian pint mug — it had to hold a exactly a pint he told a reporter later, perhaps unconscious of the conflict with one of his other enthusiams (and later responsibility) for going metric: finally the pint mug arrived — on a silver salver! The story fits very well the idea of the new broom, the no-nonsense man of the people who is going to come in and sweep away the traditional mumbo jumbo and drag an old fashioned custom-bound organsation, kicking and screaming if necessary, into the third quarter of the twentieth century. Yet, in fact, modernity is neither here nor there. The object of production is consumption and any economic enterprise should be measured by customer satisfaction. Whether it is done by traditional methods or by the most up-to-date is of little consequence. What really matters is whether the consumer is provided with a good quality, reasonably personal, service. This is not how Benn tends to view economic relationships. His whole interest seems to be concentrated at the production end of the operation, while his attitude to marketing is to see it as public relations — keeping the customer happy, not by providing him or her with what he or she wants, but by using all the most modern techniques of persuasion to induce acceptance of what is provided.

Following this ideology, an organisation like the Post Office must be made technically efficient, an aim easily equated with the acquisition of all the latest novelties — whether or not the client at the counter requires them. Regrettably, what is technically superb may be economically inefficient and the emphasis on technique in a department of government may mean the degeneration of policy into gadgetry and gimmickry. That, unhappily, is what became the most striking characteristic of Benn's first Ministry. Of course gadgets are not all bad, and many gimmicks have useful effects, but to harvest fruitful innovation requires not only enthusiasm in its launching; it needs the quality which Sir Frances Drake prayed for: a resolute patience and staying-power. Whether Benn had these qualities time would show, but he certainly had zest and not long after his arrival at the ministry he fired a salvo of 150 memos suggesting improvements. Here surely was some of the bottled-up energy which he had earlier said was in the Labour party and waiting to be applied to government!

Let us consider the problems of the GPO's different departments in turn and see what Benn contributed towards their solution. First take telephones: when Benn took over in 1964 there were mounting complaints about the long wait for a new telephone and about the poor quality of the service, especially the large number of crossed lines, delays due to half-functioning equipment and calls misdirected or blocked. Yet Benn's period of office was not notable for an attack on any of these things except perhaps the first (to which we shall come in a moment). What is best remembered is a series of headline-grabbing novelties which brought little real improvement and in one case (all figure numbers) probably added to them. One of his more publicised achievements was the introduction of a new kind of telephone which was shaped like a flat iron, and which, instead of ringing would 'warble gently like a bird'. As Colin Cross put it at the time, it was 'the sure mark of an inward-looking organisation, run for the benefit of its staff rather than the public, that it should produce such an instrument at a time when it is failing in its basic job'.

At least people did not have to have the new telephone if they did not want it, but they had to accept Benn's other innovation whether they liked it or not — all figure dialling. (As a result, Benn's own London number ceased to be Park 5503 and became 01-727 5503.) The main reason for this change was, so he said, to enable the public to dial internationally, because there would soon be 600 million telephone subscribers in the world. Yet surely that advantage could have been as easily obtained by simply giving the number for international calls and keeping PARk, WIMbledon, KENsington and all the rest of them for local calls. His other justification was that they were running out of names for exchanges because only eighty more combinations would make pronounceable names. However, as Peter Lewis pointed out at the time in the *Daily Mail,* what is wrong with unpronounceable syllables, such as GRR? And what competition there would be for SSS, BOO and YAH! More important, going over to figures did away with telephone numbers which were easy to remember. When people had to ask for their numbers from the operator, time was lost because the operator invariably asked for the number to be repeated, whereas PARk 5503 could be remembered first time. The cost of such delay must by now be enormous. Another convenience was lost too: when there was a message to ring back a number, the letters gave a clue to the place of origin of the call, whereas numbers are anonymous. It is revealing of the extent to which the people of Britain had grown apathetic and were so bemused by talk of technological revolutions that they accepted a change involving so much inconvenience just for the dubious benefit of the few who go in for international calls. In San Francisco, where all numeral dialling was first introduced, the irate citizens at least put up a fight. Their protest was led by the splendid Professor (of Semantics) Hayakawa — soon to achieve fame by his firm handling of student revolt at the San Francisco State College. He protested against the reduction of all good and treasured things to numbers simply to make them more digestible to machines: 'The passive acceptance of creeping mechanisation has gone far enough'. In fact Hayakawa and his fellow protestors succeeded only in delaying, not stopping, the onward march of all digital dialling, but it was a healthy and enviable response to social (and telephonic) engineering. Luckily for Benn there were no protestors of this calibre on hand and his wretched so-called reform went through with scarcely a dog barking or a telephone ringing.

Along with the gimmicks came the publicity. Any budding Hayakawa who did write to Benn about the deficiencies of the telephone service would have in reply a postcard apparently written by the Postmaster General himself, though in fact it was just a duplicated message. In the same way, human interest stories were fed to the press which he so affected to despise. Like the story of how 'the direct intervention of the Postmaster General who, working directly from his home, acted as a telephone operator, and enabled a British businessman to clinch a £1 million export deal'. This was all about how Benn, on reading in the newspaper that Mr Leonard Matchan (Chairman of the Cope Allmann engineering organisation) was finding it impossible to ring his office in Sydney Australia about an export order because the lines were booked with Christmas greetings messages, 'sprang into action' to save the deal. Which was, of course, admirable, but one swallow does not make a summer, and why was the system unable to cope without involving the aid of superman Benn himself? It would indeed be an odd state of affairs if the best way to remedy any fault in the telephone service were by writing to the papers in the hope that the Postmaster General might read about it.

The real winner from a publicity point of view, however, was the London Post Office Tower protruding its green glass and concrete 620 feet above Bloomsbury and right on cue for the new Postmaster General. No doubt, with its capacity to handle 150 000 simultaneous telephone calls and 40 television channels, it was an important installation. It owed nothing to Benn himself, but its inauguration in October 1965 was the most flagrant bit of ministerial self-promotion to date. The PMG made a comparison between Big Ben and the new structure which. it cowered beneath. Big Ben represented 'the fussy grandeur of the Gothic revival that epitomised Victorian Imperial affluence founded on the post industrial revolution', while the Post Office Tower 'lean, practical, futuristic, symbolises the technical and architectural skill of this new age'. Apparently his ardent hope was that a grateful and admiring populace would christen it 'Benn's Tower' but the populace did not oblige. Harold Wilson came along to open it ceremonially by using the first microwave sent out from the building in order to talk to the Lord Mayor of Birmingham. It was an historic moment, but whatever it was he said, *The Times* evidently did not think it worth mentioning.

In April 1966 there was yet another well-reported story — this time about Benn's reactions having seen a film about the microbug equipment manufactured by an American, Mr Ben Jamil, who had come over to show his apparatus at the US trade fair in Britain. One of Mr Jamil's seventy-five devices would apparently allow an industrialist in Zurich to listen to a secret board meeting of his rivals in London. Benn's response was to refuse a licence to demonstrate eavesdropping equipment and Mr Jamil was unable to show his devices at the Trade Fair. Few would quarrel with that (except to wonder a little at how it came about that a licence was needed at all!). Nobody would defend using a recording device without the knowledge of the person being recorded, though Benn had not been quite so scrupulous about recording his conversation with poor Paul Fluck of the *Western Daily Press,* but then maybe general elections are different.

A vintage example of Benn's success in public relations was an article by Quentin Crewe in the *Daily Mirror* in October 1965. Q.C. dwelt in his column on the theme of 'why did I ever go and see Benn and tax him with the inefficiency of the Post Office'? It turned out that Benn had a file in front of him which enabled him to answer all the columnist's grumbles with all manner of cryptic facts such as:

> 'Telephone bills: at present 800 million trunk calls have to be billed. Full details of each would be prohibitively expensive.'

> 'Inland Directory enquiries: Average time to answer, 20 seconds.'

As for all-figure dialling, Benn — by now the fully fledged paternalist — said that Crewe would have to accept that the reasons were good ones which would mean a more efficient service:

> 'If you see a doctor, you accept advances in medicine even if they seem more complicated than old-fashioned remedies. All-number dialling may seem an intrusion into a quiet life, but it is progress. You can dial more people. Get more out of your telephone.'

All these bold and questionable assertions were allowed to pass without a peep out of Crewe, who perhaps enjoyed presenting himself as the simpleton, an attitude which also had the merit of being more interesting journalistically than a straightforward tribute to Benn's efficiency — which however sincere might look like a straight public relations puff. In any case, Crewe probably was both impressed and out of his depth, fascinated but also cowed by all the apparatus and expertise being thrown at him and it was presumably *Mirror* policy to give Benn the benefit of the doubt.

These few examples merely serve to illustrate how Benn projected a favourable image of himself as the go-go technocrat who had become everyone's friendly neighbourhood Postmaster General, but what about the customers? That story was rather less heroic. One thing Benn could and did claim was that during his last year as PMG a record 808 000 new telephones were installed, though the waiting list actually doubled. Yet it seems likely that, assuming that this was attributable to his new broom activity, it was a case of concentrating on the recruitment of new subscribers at the expense of service to the old. As Benn said in a report to Parliament on 3 August 1965 '... if priority were given to existing customers the waiting list would probably have risen'. He also said that congestion would become worse before it improved. This looked very like a case of priority for the most quantifiable improvement and the one most easily projected and sloganised at the cost of quality, which is less easy to present from a propaganda point of view. In this case it so happens, however, that it is possible to show how awful the telephone service actually was during the period when Benn was responsible. For one thing, the Post Office's own figures, revealed in a parliamentary question on 3 August 1965, showed that the call failure rate was at a record high during 1964-5 (which included part of Benn's first year as PMG), the trunk call failure rate being twice the average for the period since 1951. What objective evidence we have suggests that the position steadily worsened during the rest of his time in the PMG's office; for example, the consumer magazine *Which* reported in July 1966 the results of a two-week exercise by 500 private subscribers on sixty-three typical exchanges throughout the country. The report showed that one in ten of 8000 attempted calls went wrong and that about one in five STD calls was faulty. This was a very thorough, painstaking analysis, but it is possible that it was unduly favourable to the GPO and that the true position was worse, since a one-day investigation by the *Sun* newspaper in February 1966 found a fault rate of seventeen per fifty calls, and if one included the cases where there was more than one fault per call, the fault rate rose to nearly twenty out of every fifty, or forty per cent! If that was a sample of the new Britain being forged in the white heat of the technological revolution, most people would have preferred the horse and buggy version. Although the overall cost of such spectacular inefficiency is probably impossible to compute, some indication was given in an estimate made by Ford Motors, which showed that 'the call failure rate was costing the company £750 a week in operatives' wasted time'. Similarly, at the Paris Air Show in 1965 delays of several hours on lines between London and Paris were said to have severely impeded sales.

In the light of all this, Benn's announcement in June 1966 which implied that telephone usage was expanding — in the previous year there had been eight per cent more local, fourteen per cent more trunk and twenty-two per cent more overseas calls — does not impress. For a start the local calls rose at the same rate as the growth of subscribers. Against higher percentages for the other types of call we should discount the total number of calls that went wrong but were invoiced, since only a minority of subscribers have the time and the persistence to claim back for every call that goes adrift. It is possible therefore that the high failure rate led to a lower effective utilisation of telephones. Yet in a way this was the nub of the matter because telephone capacity was seriously under-used in Britain compared with other countries — it was at this stage only a fifth of that in the United States.

Telephone charges rose sharply just after Benn moved on

Top: Father and son (and friend) in June 1946. Left to right: William Wedgwood Benn, Lord Stansgate; William Dobbie, Labour MP for Rotherham; Tony Benn. *(Sport and General Press Agency)*

Bottom: Stepping out. The Hydrogen Bomb National Campaign committee with a 1954 petition calling for summit talks on arms control. Left to right: Sidney Silverman MP, the Rev. Dr Donald (now Lord) Soper; Anthony Greenwood MP and Tony Benn MP. *(Press Association Photos)*

Top: The reluctant peer. Hilary (aged 7) and Julian (aged 9) help their father with some of the ninety-one law books used in his fight to renounce the Stansgate peerage. *(Associated Newspapers Group Limited)*

Bottom: The ex-peer. Caroline and Tony Benn display their renunciation of the Stansgate peerage. *(Central Press Photos)*

from the Post Office, and though these were part of the emergency package of economic increases in the Labour government's financial crisis in July 1966, the Post Office report which came out — curiously enough on the very same day as the increases were announced — indicated that charges would in any case have had to rise. And rise they did, the domestic telephone charge jumping from £3.50 to £4.00, the connection charge was doubled (from £10 to £20), while all new telephone subscribers had to pay a year's instead of a quarter's rental in advance. The deterioration of this increasingly costly telephone service was said by Benn to be due to 'the consistent under-capitalisation from which it has suffered over the past forty years'. But why was the lack of capital chronic? The plausible answer is that this was a result of its being a nationalised monopoly in which capital tended to be allocated to government activities according to their political popularity or glamour, not according to their commercial soundness. As a result, the usual financial competitive pressure did not apply. The urge to go out and sell the service was not there — a report by the Post Office Engineering Union in 1961 had said 'the Post Office has used its specialist sales staff mainly to explain why service cannot be provided'. A capital shortage did indeed limit the capacity of the telephone system and it would have been counter-productive to advertise a service if it was already in short supply. However, if there is an unfilled demand, it should be possible to make a profit by satisfying it, in which case any capital necessary could be raised at a commercial rate of interest. In the United States there is a virtual private monopoly in the hands of the American Telephone and Telegraph (holding) Company, which is watched over by a Public Utility Commission. It is generally acknowledged that the American telephone service is excellent and it is five times as intensively used by subscribers as the British system. The coverage of the population is so extensive that canvassing in US elections is done on the telephone — which would be disastrous in the UK — and customer relations are first-rate.

Admittedly, it was Benn's job to run an already nationalised industry and he could not be blamed for its inherent faults, but it remains a fact that he was the most ardent of nationalisers and eager to extend the Post Office's empire whenever possible.

The oldest part of the Post Office was of course the post. Here again his period as Minister coincided with a great deal of gimmickry and publicity while the service declined and charges went up. Nearly a year after Benn's appointment the Post Office mounted an exhibition in London showing how it was adapting itself to the age of automation. There was what were called 'robot postmen'—'These ingenious machines, flickering with ultraviolet lights, purring with a Martian hum, can read addresses and sort letters as swiftly as an army of educated octopods'. One of them, for instance could sort 20 000 letters an hour. All very fine, but a good deal of what was to be accomplished by these machines depended on postal coding. This was analogous to — but from the customer's point of view potentially a good deal worse than — the all-figure telephone numbers and another example of the trend towards inconveniencing people for the sake of making data more digestible to machines. And is it entirely unreasonable for people to feel apprehensive at the thought that there may come a time when they will not be able to write to their loved ones unless they know the wretched postal code? Even if they are willing, will their memories let them down or will they copy it correctly? Yet Benn was full of plans — and he had already two months earlier announced a £25 million programme of mechanisation which, he declared, would 'revolutionise the postal service'.

Another minor postal revolution was happening to stamps. Until Benn arrived, the Post Office had been conservative almost to the point of stuffiness about commemorative issues. It was only banana republics and one or two big countries, anxious to increase foreign currency earnings from sales to stamp collectors — Nazi Germany was an outstanding example — which produced legions of new stamps. British stamps were instantly recognisable, dignified and a little dull. Benn wanted to brighten them up and in his first twelve months be brought out nine 'specials', compared with only five special issues during the whole period between the wars, and two of those were for royal occasions — a jubilee and a coronation. After Benn got to work it was not long before there was even a stamp with dog roses, honey suckle and a fanciful water-lily to commemorate the tenth Botanical Congress. On the whole, it was probably one of the better things Benn did, as it added to the sense of innocent pleasure. According to Stanley Gibbons, the world's largest stamp dealing firm, the number of stamp collectors increased fourfold during those twelve months, and the philatelic bureau especially set up to meet needs of collectors made £500 000. There were one or two rows. On one occasion a stamp was issued on 13 September to commemorate the twenty-fifth anniversary of the Battle of Britain. Of unusually bad design, it showed British planes flying over the shattered tail fin of a *Luftwaffe* bomber that had been shot down and on the tail fin was a broken swastika. This symbol of Nazism upset the Jewish community, there were protests from the Board of British Jews and questions were asked in Parliament, but Benn refused to withdraw the stamp. He also produced a stamp in honour of Churchill, but it took months to get ready and the absurd situation arose that the American stamp appeared before the British issue.

Also in his first year Benn cut postal deliveries in some parts of London from three to two per day and pulled back by half an hour the time for the last collection. These reductions in customer services must have contributed to the delays about which there was much complaint in the letter columns of the newspapers. Again in 1965 he made permanent the three-year suspension of deliveries on Christmas Day. The special Christmas airmail stamp brought out that year was generally considered to be poor compensation.

Of all Benn's activities in this department his most notable achievement was the introduction of the fourpenny post — it had been three pence — and he did not have the stamps ready for the dearer issue. Arguably, this price increase was unnecessary; the letter post was being used to subsidise the parcel post which should have been increased instead. It was the biggest price increase of 1965 and coincided with the government's strenuous attempt — alas, one of many to come — to stabilise prices and wages. Absorbed in his gimmicks, Benn failed to exploit opportunities for profit. In April 1965, for example, he cancelled the delivery of unaddressed printed matter (the household delivery service) which had begun in January the previous year and was already making around £300 000 a year. Why did he drop it? Because of pressure from the Union of Post Office Workers who insisted that the delivery of an unaddressed letter required no skill and therefore lowered the postman's status — an excellent example of how the British status game (which the unions now play more enthusiastically than anyone else) reduced productivity, making the rest of us poor.

In short, Benn never got to the crux of the matter which was that the postal service needed to be decentralised — ideally it should have lost its statutory monopoly so that rival postal services, run by milk delivery firms for instance, could start up in competition. The best move open to him as a socialist would have been to give more independence to local head postmasters to make a profit, allowing them for example, to boost business by making reductions in charges for local post — which accounts for nearly one letter in every three. (See *The Postal Service, Competition or Monopoly?* by Ian Senior, Institute of Economic Affairs, 1970.)

It was Benn who first announced the Post Office's plans for the Post Office bank, the Giro. This was a credit transfer system imitated from the continent where it had been in operation since before World War 1. In Britain, with a much more widely used banking system — twenty-seven per cent of the working population with bank accounts — the need was far from obvious, but those Tory MPs who urged caution were sharply told by Benn that their party had been too negative in their approach to the Giro when they were in power. He extolled the new system on the grounds that it would improve national savings, cut down crime, and save manpower. However, it is not unreasonable to suspect that as far as Benn was concerned the great attraction was the establishment in government hands of a workers' bank and one which could compete strongly with the clearing banks — though they, incidentally, had promised to co-operate fully. It would also provide employment in Merseyside, which was good electorally and give a boost to the computer industry, fitting in nicely with the technological revolution idea which Labour was constantly seeking to promote. In fact Giro did not start in business until 1968, but after exposure to Benn its destiny was already clear: one, it would receive lots of publicity, and two, it would lose lots of money.

As Postmaster General, Benn was overlord of broadcasting. This was unfortunate because, though personally benefitting greatly from media publicity, he was very sensitive to criticism and like his master, Harold Wilson, deeply suspicious of bias (if not to the same extent) against the Labour party or himself. Wilson showed his attitude at the 1965 Labour conference after the BBC gave Clive Jenkins, a leading trade union critic of the Government's incomes policy, an opportunity to spout his opinions in an interview with Robin Day. As a result, Paul Fox, the BBC producer responsible for current affairs, was summoned to Wilson's room and was given a rocket. The producer was warned 'to mend his ways or the Government would have to think of ways of bringing the BBC under tighter discipline'. A Labour spokesman said that the complaints ranged much wider than this incident, and that the *Gallery* programme, for instance, had become nothing but a party political broadcast for the Tories. This followed on the heels of another minor row when George Wigg, the Paymaster-General, had tried to pressurise the BBC into allowing George Brown to make a series of so-called 'non-partisan' speeches in the course of the month before the launching of the National Plan. The BBC refused for the excellent reason that the National Plan was not a non-partisan document. There then followed Labour complaints that the BBC was being partisan. The whole controversy was eventually defused after a meeting of the party leaders which agreed on a formula defining policy in political broadcasting and the opposition right of reply.

It was three years later, after he had left the PMG post that Benn fully vented his decidedly intolerant views on the relationship between the broadcaster and the politician. His problem at this juncture was what to do about 'pirate' radio. The word 'pirate' is emotive of course and was used to cast aspersions on the private enterprise Radio Caroline and Radio London which had been established on vessels outside British territorial waters. They were therefore not infringing the BBC radio's statutory monopoly which at that time only applied to the British Isles. Absurdly enough, the only law which could be held to apply to them was one which restricted the radio receiving licence issued by the Postmaster General to the reception of messages from authorised broadcasting stations. Listening to unlicensed broadcasts was an offence under the Wireless Telegraphy Act of 1949 which was aimed mainly at preventing people from tuning in to police calls. The law provided for a fine on first offence of £10 rising to £50 on subsequent offences. Obviously such a law could only be enforced in a totalitarian state. Besides, the pirate stations were well liked. They provided cheery programmes of pop music introduced by disc jockeys with an easy-going style and pleasant personalities, and they were extremely popular. By the end of 1965, indeed, it was widely assumed that the Government would accept the facts of life and license them to operate on the mainland. Benn was rather enraged at any such idea and issued a statement repudiating the suggestion that he would do any such thing. His statement continued, 'Earlier this year Britain signed the European Convention, committing itself to legislation that would outlaw these stations broadcasting on frequencies allocated to other stations in Europe'. This sounded all very authoritative and as if some international law was involved.

There   indeed been an international agreement before, the 1948 Copenhagen Plan sponsored by the thirty-two countries belonging to the European Broadcasting Union, but in the end only twenty-five of them signed it, and by 1964 *Wireless World* pointed out in an editorial that 'more than fifty per cent of long wave and medium wave broadcasting stations in Europe are at present operating on frequencies other than those allocated by the Copenhagen Plan'. The truth was that such broadcasting agreements had hardly ever worked, so why pick on the pirates? In addition, keeping these companies off the air was a denial of freedom comparable with the suppression of privately owned newspapers (though as we shall see Benn could not be accused on inconsistency there because he *did* believe that newspapers should be subject to a form of workers' censorship). Nor was there any serious shortage of wavelengths; the medium band was more fully occupied than it might have been, very largely because the British government — with little consideration for the listening public or the other signatories of the wavelength sharing agreement already referred to — had occupied it, rather than the relative band, with air beacons. Benn's reference in his speech therefore to the causing of interference on the continent and the potential danger to ship to shore transmissions was to be taken with several grains of salt. (The occasion when the FBI Agents looking after President Carter on his trip to Paris in 1977 had their conversations transmitted on the same wavelength as the chorus of the Folies Bergère should not be taken as typical.) In any event, for all these bogus reasons Benn promised to introduce legislation as soon as was practicable, and he gave a categorical assurance that there was no future for the pirate radio stations. He must have been a little surprised at the immediate sequel — though he should not have been if he knew that the combined audience of the pirates was 20 million people — for he was flooded with letters protesting against his proposal to ban them, and Benn took the crucial step of writing to each correspondent personally, explaining why he was going to take them off the air. He in fact handed out the bogus explanation about the pirates taking over other countries' wavelengths. It is curious that the proprietors of the pirate stations themselves did not appreciate that in Benn they were dealing with a closed mind totally hostile to any policy which would allow private enterprise to expand into the territory of a state corporation, regardless of the effect on the service. They still went on talking (like the spokesman of Radio City for instance) as if it was only a matter of time before they were land-based and legitimate.

Finally, it will come as no surprise after seeing how Benn operated in the rest of his GPO 'empire' to learn that in broadcasting too he raised the charges. On 14 April 1965 he raised the combined sound and television licence fee from £4 to £5 and the fee for sound only from £1 to £1.25.

To be fair to Benn one should not blame him for not solving the problems of the Post Office in two years. It is far too big an organisation to be run by one man, let alone a Minister whose main talents and training are political. That Benn realised some of the problems is shown by his recommendation that the Post Office should be turned into a corporation and run on commercial lines. In a speech in October 1965 he argued that the old civil service tradition in the GPO should give way to a more flexible approach. However, if what he really wanted was a less bureaucratic Post Office, simply making it into a corporation solved very little as it then became like the other nationalised corporations — that is to say, not answerable to Parliament on detailed performance. From the democratic point of view, therefore, turning the Post Office into a corporation was surely a retrograde step. While the Post Office remained the size it was, and while it remained so centralised, it could not but be bureaucratic. Then as now, the Post Office needed to be broken up. This would have involved hiving off the telephone side of the business, even splitting it up into independent areas, and in the case of letter and parcel post, allowing head postmasters to run their own local show, while at the same time abolishing the postal monopoly. If such charges would have been distasteful to Benn then they would be abhorrent to the Benn of today.

This period in Benn's life may have done credit to his energy but his romanticised view of technology as the servant of man was, if anything, a hindrance to reform. For it led to a diversion of energies from the main task of reducing costs and taking more account of market forces as a guide by reforming the price structure, not just raising charges across the board when there was a cost-cutting panic at the Treasury. However, if judged as a businessman, Benn was not a successful Postmaster General, he had his successes as a politician in projecting himself and his ideas, however superficial and trendy they might be. It was this capacity for self-projection, however, which appealed to Wilson, who was no businessman either (except when it came to selling his own books) and which commended Benn in his eyes. According to the Crossman diaries, Wilson later said of Benn that though he talked nonsense outside his ministry, 'When he's on the job he talks sense'. The PM was not an especially shrewed judge of character — and he may have been swayed by the feeling that Benn was very similar to himself, sharing probably more than any of the other Ministers Wilson's schoolboyish enthusiasm for technology and his fond hopes of its providing a solution to all our problems. Better still, Benn was equipped with the oratorical talent to maintain the illusion. Thus it was because Wilson found his personality and approach so congenial that Benn must have seemed the natural candidate for promotion in July 1966. Frank Cousins, the trade union boss, whom Wilson had made Minister of Technology, had been rather a flop. Coming to the Commons late in life, he was subtly unadaptable to its ways. And no wonder, for after being the leader of Britain's largest union — the Transport and General Workers — he was not accustomed to the irreverent treatment which the

Commons is accustomed to give to its own. Besides, like almost all leading unionists, he had spent a lifetime resisting the impact of technology, not encouraging it. It was not surprising that Wilson should turn to his still youthful disciple and place the Ministry so crucial to Labour's plans in his hands. For Benn in a sense it would be like going home, because the Ministry building at Millbank was on the site of the house where he was born, and where he had lived from 1925 to 1949. It had been demolished some years before to make way for the new office building. What new structures would Benn build at his new office?

4

WEDG BENN OF MIN TECH

1966~8

The immediate reason for Frank Cousins' decision to leave the Government, and as it turned out, make way for Benn, was his total disagreement with its incomes policy. For one whose whole career had been made within the framework of free collective bargaining, the idea of a three and a half per cent norm for wage increases was, as he said in his letter of resignation 'fundamentally wrong', and the Prices and Incomes Bill 'meaningless'. The *Sun* described the resignation as 'sensational' and 'the most devastating act of its kind since Aneurin Bevan walked out of the Attlee cabinet in 1951'. This was a rather extravagant comparison; Cousins was a figure of consequence, not like Bevan because of his talent and charisma, but because he had been made to look larger than life by his position as boss of Britain's biggest union. The issue he raised about the impropriety and fatuity of an incomes policy was indeed very pertinent, but ran counter to the conventional wisdom of the time. Even so, as a man deeply committed to the goal of a wholly socialist state, he was hardly the right person to object. For it is only within a mainly capitalist social order that the system of collective bargaining — which belongs to the market economy, not to the command economy of socialism — can continue. Yet his natural instinct as an old union man was sound, for the traditional character and independence of trade unions could not survive under a government wage dictatorship. Under such a regime the only role left for the unions was that of government agencies — precisely what they are in the Soviet Union. Newcomer Benn was a useful contrast to Cousins. As opposed to his predecessor who (especially at question time) appeared grey, bumbling and cantankerous, Benn was pink faced and full of zest and charm. The zest was especially in evidence on the very morning of his arrival at his new office, where he arrived at 8.00 am — two full hours before Cousins rolled up to greet him as the old incumbent welcoming the new.

How did Britain's next-to-youngest cabinet Minister (Richard Marsh at thirty-eight was two years younger) view his new job? He was not the one to miss his chance of expounding that! He told a London *Evening News* reporter that he had a responsibility for stimulating the productivity side of the prices and incomes policy. This was an attractive role, for it implied that while the other Ministers were engaged, one way or another, in holding down wages, he was the one who, with deft technological stimulus, was jacking up productivity, and swelling the cornucopia of goods which those wages would buy. It all sounded splendidly straightforward: Benn's finger on the button, as it were, and production would leap up like a spring lamb. The young dynamic forward-looking swinging image of the new Minister was helped on by his wife, Caroline, who appeared at a reception given by the Foreign Secretary for Premier Pompidou of France at Lancaster House, wearing a white afternoon dress four inches above the knee, white lace stockings, no hat and no gloves. From all accounts someone quite innocently mistook her for one of the twenty-one-year-old Jay twins. She wore an equally swinging outfit the following February when attending an official reception for Mr Kosygin, the Soviet Premier, during his eight-day visit to Britain.

Benn was in his element. His understanding of technology was not greater than that of the average reader of the *New Scientist,* but his capacity for oracular pronouncement about its new horizons was second to none. His real flair, now as ever, was primarily verbal and concerned with the images which words can produce. Thus a visit to Fords at Dagenham to see the millionth Cortina roll off the production lines, had him coming up with a characteristic catch phrase, 'The Battle of Britain 1966 must be won on the parking lots of America' — a fine contemporary wrapping for the weary old exhortation to export more cars to the United States. At the opening of a new Industrial Training Board at Bristol, his way of putting across the trite, if also true, notion that education should continue throughout life was to say that the television hero Dr Finlay would be a menace if he were alive today because he had the idea — not in fact true, as Finley buffs will recall — that the skill acquired at the beginning of his life would last him the rest of his days. When talking to a national productivity conference he put forward the arresting idea that by better lubrication throughout industry Britain might save over five to seven years as much as £500 million. This was very possibly true, though like many other simple prescriptions for our ills it might amount in the end to just one more form of monomania — Mao Tse Tung had the same sort of obsession about pushing forward the Chinese economy by simply insisting that every wheel in China should have a rubber tyre!

Benn's supreme gift lay in the advertising skills which he so affected to despise. Although the Ministry of Technology was in reality an administrative rag-bag stuffed with departments which did not fit anywhere else, Benn was the ideal man to make it appear that a silk purse could be made out of such a sow's ear. So when any equally earnest spirit, like Joe Rogaly of *The Financial Times* went to see him to enquire about the inner light which guided the Minister towards the promised land of technologically contrived affluence, Benn was always ready with a sort of WEA lecture: how history was changing things before our very eyes, how we were careering away from the century after 1850 when the British were training their lads in public schools to become District Commissioners or Viceroys in the jolly old empire and of how in the new age of socialist enlightenment, we had comprehensive schools, no empire and a recognition that, in answer to Dean Acheson (Britain has lost an empire but not yet found a role), 'Britain's new role is industrial excellence'. It was all dazzlingly superficial and the analogy at first sight so compelling that few could be expected to pause and consider that while the public schools did produce colonial administrators (though this was only a negligible proportion of their total output), the comprehensive schools were already doing an outstandingly feeble job of producing likely contributors to the nation's excellence in industrial or any other spheres — as the first *Black Paper* which appeared about eighteen months later so devastatingly showed.

Benn's projectionist talent was revealed in what even the *Daily Telegraph* headlined as a 'hypnotic' television programme by Benn in a party political broadcast in October 1966. In fact the headline proved to be satirical for the correspondent turned out to be not so much hypnotised as fascinated by the way Benn fixed the viewers 'with a wide-eyed glittering stare, as if defying them to switch off'. Benn's generally cheery discourse on the joys which the technological future had in store did nevertheless include one expression of regret, though entirely at the expense of his political opponents, when he gave voice to the lament, 'If only the Ministry of Technology had been set up ten years ago, if only the work we are now engaged in, which is bound to take some time before it comes to full fruition, had been started in time. What a very different prospect this country would now have.' All very affecting no doubt, but also very speculative and based on little more than optimism and departmental prejudice. Of hard evidence pointing in that direction there was none.

Not that qualms about such details would ever have been likely to staunch the flow of technomanic propaganda for which his new post provided so ideal an outlet. Thus in November he was on hand to announce his list of the top ten Britons, from which he modestly excluded himself, and indeed all politicians, and (naturally) 'colonial administrators, diplomats and the Establishment top brass'. Instead, just as predictably, they proved to be engineers, managers and salesmen. He also set up a six-man committee to study the brain drain — always a good subject for newspaper articles.

In his early days as Minister, Benn's enthusiasm for technology was so ardent that it eclipsed his passion for socialism. He was even to be heard urging that firms should be profitable, that the mixed economy continue for as far ahead as we could see and that ownership mattered less than technology. This was much to the distaste of the *Morning Star* (which normally gave him a good press) and which was particularly irked with the Benn theory — had he been talking to his old tutor Anthony Crosland? — that 'capitalism in Britain has evolved new ways' and that socialism was changing too, with public enterprise 'the fertiliser of, and participant in, economic growth, and not only in terms of nationalisation, of existing concerns'. He even suggested that the new technology had brought a new 'common interest between government and industry'.

The Chrysler takeover of Rootes in March 1967 might be said to reflect this mixed economy philosophy, though there was in fact less philosophy about it than expediency. From the point of view of preserving jobs the appearance of a big American car-maker ready to carry on (but with much larger resources) where the old British company had left off was a godsend. The only problem was political — Labour had opposed the Conservative decision to allow Chrysler to buy into Rootes in 1963. The Labour Left indeed, preferred nationalisation. Michael Foot in particular asked indignantly how Britain could send troops all over the world while finding it impossible to control her motor industry at home. Not everyone would have said the two were necessarily connected, but the answer if not the question was clear. Nationalisation would pre-empt funds from other projects at a time of financial stringency. The rival claims of doctrine and expediency were reconciled in a deal by which Chrysler was allowed to extend its holding in Rootes, provided that fifteen percent of Rootes' equity capital was held by other shareholders. The Industrial Reorganisation Corporation (an independent government agency for restructuring industry which had one of Benn's advisers on the board) then took up a holding of this size, investing £1 662 228 in the company and in consequence was entitled to nominate one shareholder to the board. It looked like an historic compromise between doctrinaire nationalisation and American money.

Meanwhile Benn's Ministry grew even larger since in November 1966 it was decided that it should absorb Aviation, i.e. research, development and procurement of aircraft, guided weapons and electronic equipment. However, it was hard to see what point there was in thus bringing so many scientists and engineers under one roof except on the dubious principle that bigness is best, nor did this annexation mark the limit of his aspirations. Not content with a ministerial empire which controlled nearly half Britain's total expenditure on research and development (£325 million out of a grand total of £750 million) and the employment of 10 000 scientists and engineers, in February 1967 Benn started a campaign to control the three contracting consortia in the nuclear plant construction industry. This he sought to do by giving the Atomic Energy Authority, which he controlled, the right to withold from the consortia the fruits of its research which up to that point they had been free to put to commercial use. This right to pick and choose as to which consortium should have access to which developments, would, so the theory went, give the AEA sufficient leverage to enable it to freeze out two of the three plant makers and nationalise the third. The AEA then would become the sole contractor to the Central Electricity Generating Board.

Benn saw himself, as he told one journalist, as 'a national entrepreneur, helping to turn the nation's assets into cash'. In other words, equipped with massive research and development funds, and with the Industrial Reconstruction Corporation acting as a sort of family merchant bank, he was in the position to do on a vastly larger scale what every shareholder is trying to do with his portfolio — to pick winners. (This is precisely how Benn defined the task of Min Tech in a speech to the American Chamber of Commerce in February 1967: 'Its (Min Tech's) aim is clear: pick likely winners and back them to the hilt with everything that is available, including money'.)

All investers however have their quirks and Benn was no exception. In these early months at the Ministry he soon showed a marked preference for supporting projects with glamour — the kinds of undertakings which would appeal to one whose favourite reading was Jules Verne and the *Guinness Book of Records* rather than the *Stock Exchange Year Book* and *Practical Mechanics*. It was thus inevitable that he should back electric car research, which not only had overtones of *Dr Who* about it, but also had the extra advantage of its appeal as a non-pollutive vehicle to the environmentalist lobby, which at this time was starting to make itself heard. Again, it was no matter for surprise when it was announced in January 1969 that the Hovercraft research previously concentrated at an experimental station in Hythe, Kent and employing fifty engineers and technicians was to be taken over and financed by his ministry. It was this interest in novelty, plus his tendency to have his feet planted firmly in mid-air, which led to his acquiring the nickname 'Hover Benn'. The reaction to his enthusiasm from his colleagues was not invariably rapturous. In her very lively book *Inside Number Ten* Marcia Williams (now Lady Falkender) recalls how at a major policy meeting,

> 'in the middle of summing up what technology
> could do to change the face of Britain, he (Benn)
> suddenly went off at a tangent and tried to enthuse
> us with the idea of the electric car. We might, he
> said, find ourselves commuting in electrically
> powered vehicles and parking them at meters,
> where we would plug them into the electricity
> generating system, and, while we were working
> away in our offices, our cars would be recharged,
> and when we leapt out again into our vehicles, they
> would be fully powered, ready to shoot off, to
> either our urban renewed home or our dwelling in
> the commuter belt.'

He certainly had what she calls 'the almost childlike gift for
seeing the excitement and the possibility of the science fiction
future'. This was an unusually kindly view from one who was
in any case well disposed to Benn, though even she, in
discussing the possibility that he might one day become
Labour's leader and conceding that he was of the right age
and of great ability, significantly voiced the doubt as to
whether the labour movement and British people 'would be
willing to repose their confidence in someone so visionary'.
That remained to be seen, but one who was not too contented
with Benn's winner-picking ability was his senior colleague
Dick Crossman who, in his diary (on 11 May 1968), dwelt on
'the lack of success of the interventionist policies of Peter
Shore and Tony Wedgwood Benn, young men who, with a
carefree arrogance, think they can enter the business world
and help it to be more efficient. It's the amateurishness of
Harold and his bright young men which gets me down.'

However, as 1967 began it looked — on the economic front
at least — like a year for the young men. For the old, or
anyway some of them, were being discarded or shunted
elsewhere, with Frank Cousins retired in a huff and George

Brown, his National Plan dead as soon as published, already shaping up for a transfer to foreign affairs.

On 15 February the *Guardian,* in an editorial said that Min Tech, which had proved disappointing since its founding amidst high hopes in 1964, was acquiring a clearer sense of direction under Benn and with Aviation coming under its wing it was experiencing a great increase in size and potential power. The editorial took comfort from the fact that the whole of engineering was together under one umbrella, and that the industry was the largest employer of engineers and scientists. Yet, it argued, this direct power which increased control of the purse-strings, touched mainly shipbuilding and aircraft. Elsewhere the Minister could only operate indirectly and on a much smaller scale, through agencies like the National Research Development Corporation. He still had no effective say over the huge sums spent by nationalised industries. That was true, but such a summing-up underestimated Benn's power to intervene at will in private industry as problems arose, or indeed according to a pre-determined plan; yet for consistent effective intervention — for good or ill — there must be, as the *Guardian* editorial suggested, a sense of direction: what American generals involved in World War 2 used to call an 'overall strategic objective', that is a philosophy. Though he did a good deal of expository speech-making, at this stage it was difficult to establish whether Benn had any really consistent point of view or whether he was like Heraclitus's river — something which changes each time we step in. The opening statement from the new enlarged Ministry which he made to John Gale, who interviewed him for the *Observer,* was a palpable publicity hit if nothing else. 'I'm interested in technology spiritually because it liberates the mind,' he said memorably, if rather obscurely. This liberation occurred mainly, it appeared, through enabling people to fulfil themselves more easily by removing the humdrum of drudgery and routine. It was very quotable but did not amount to a policy. A more operationally important part of the statement was its almost unqualified acceptance of the gospel of size, of the idea that bigness is best: 'Everything's getting bigger. Schools are getting bigger, local government's getting bigger, super-powers are the big powers.' With such faith in gigantism surely he would be in favour of encouraging larger industrial groupings and giving mergers the go-ahead?

However, there were other possibly conflicting criteria which emerged in the course of 1967. There was the belief in high, or advanced, technology; there was the attachment to the idea of modernisation, the adoption of metrication being an example. During Wilson's short-lived attempt to enter the Common Market Benn was converted to the belief in a European Technological Community — another aspect of the theme of the bigger the better. He became excited at different times about the importance of profitability, and at others the need to avoid pushing profits to excess. Often he talked of picking winners, but an ailing industry in an electorally crucial part of the country, where a rise in unemployment might damage the Labour vote, could generally rely on his support. Was there any other link then but expediency? It is hard to say without looking at examples.

Chief among the old industries in need of salvage was shipbuilding, for which a Bill was published in February 1967. This sought to reorganise the shipyards into bigger units under a Shipbuilding Board as had been recommended by the Geddes Committee in March the previous year. The Board was to inject into the industry £12.5 million of working capital, £15 million for new projects, and £5 million for grants to meet transitional losses. As an additional inducement to reorganise, the Government was to guarantee loans of up to £200 million to shipowners for orders placed in Britain. Whether after taking the money the shipbuilding industry would really reorganise into bigger units or whether if it did so, that would improve its efficiency — weakened as it was by restrictive practices enforced by a variety of unions — remained to be seen. *The Financial Times* warned editorially,

'The risk in Mr Benn's decision is that credit will be made available too easily, that uncompetitive firms will be kept in existence longer than otherwise and that the nationalisation of the industry will be hampered and delayed. It would have been better to wait until reorganisation had gone further before producing this succulent carrot.'

It was hardly encouraging that one of the first exercises in support in April was to help the Firth of Clyde Big Dock Company keep its £4 million dock in working order while hoping that some kindly consortium of shipbuilders would make a bid.

The aircraft industry also had a long tradition of working hand in glove with, or more accurately hand in the wallet of the Government, and June found Benn announcing that he was continuing to provide finance for Short Brothers, the Belfast firm, which had contracts, either already in hand or in the final stages of negotiation, for the Short Skyvan light aircraft, worth £7 million. It was said to have a good chance of selling 400 skyvans to North America over the next decade. The strange thing was that Shorts had been found guilty by Ministry investigators only a month earlier of making an excess profit of around £1½ million on its Royal Navy contracts for the Seacat missile. Apparently the rate of profit allowed by Min Tech was seven and a half per cent whereas the firm had had the temerity to make thirty per cent by selling to foreign navies and thus extending the production run. This was not quite in the class of the revelation in 1964 of the eighty-two per cent profit made by Ferranti on its Bloodhound missile, but it was high enough to be an embarrassment to Benn — especially since Short's had already borrowed £2 000 000 from the Ministry of Aviation which Mr Mulley, then Minister, told the House in January 1968 was to help the firm start producing Skyvans. Many MPs became most agitated at the thought that Short's had profited so much and let it be known that they would press

Benn to make a statement after Parliament returned from recess. To make the whole thing more laughable, the Government actually had sixty-nine and a half per cent stake in the company. Benn's response was to press in turn for the dismissal of the Chairman, fifty-nine year old Mr Cuthbert Wrangham, who it was reported first heard of his dismissal, from reading the newspaper, and after confirming it, tendered his resignation. This, however evoked a uninamous protest from the company's nine directors, who at a special meeting in London on 21 June expressed their opposition in a whole-hearted vote of confidence in Mr Wrangham, and voiced their concern for the company 'to which he has made an outstanding contribution'. Benn however overruled them, denied that there had been any leak about the decision to replace Mr Wrangham and stuck to his decision. Apparently Mr Wrangham had displeased him the year before because when he was advised to take his firm out of the aircraft industry and to diversify into other small engineering activities he had refused, and if Benn's subsequent support of his Skyvan made any sense at all, he had been proved right. That was undoubtedly his big mistake. Certainly, nothing in this confused episode suggested that, for all his posturing, Benn was the stuff that tycoons are made of, except perhaps in his insistence on having his own way. Benn undoubtedly had a point when he spoke to Britain's plane makers at the end of June and accused former aviation Ministers of 'running off with sums of money that made the Great Train Robbers look like schoolboys pinching pennies from a blindman's purse', but he was hardly the one to make it. Indeed, the promise in the same speech that the Government would get tougher about sinking taxpayers' cash into aircraft projects unless they showed a profit was in itself welcome. Those words however came oddly from the lips of the Minister who was responsible for backing Concorde, the sums spent on which really did make the Great Train Robbery look like stealing the petty cash.

In the following month, as if to add insult to financial

injury, Benn gave orders for sonic bang trials to test public reaction to Concorde. So, at 3.29 pm on 17 July, London had its first supersonic bang. Within minutes the Ministry of Technology was flooded with complaints. Evidently people did not like being treated as guinea-pigs. At 4.00 pm there was apparently an hour-long queue of telephone callers wishing to speak to the Concorde department in St Giles Court in Central London. Benn was himself in his glass tower at Millbank at the time and admitted that he heard the bang, but declined to give his reaction. A sound engineer in London measured 130 decibels and the Chairman of the Noise Abatement Society, John Connell, said that babies had been woken up and people were complaining of 'tremendous shock'. Benn calmly announced, 'The Government will have to decide whether higher intensity tests should be initiated in the light of the results of the current series'. The bangs were made by a Lightning aircraft and were intended to simulate what Concorde would produce. When asked by Ivor Richard how much worse than the recent explosions the real thing would be, Benn said 'It is no good us saying that we want other people to buy the aircraft and fly it over this country if we are not prepared to see whether some mild supersonic flights over the United Kingdom are tolerable'. That was an evasion, or at any rate an answer to a different, if related, question 'Why have them at all', the answer being, 'To sell Concorde'. Yet, even if Concorde *did* sell, the bangs were another entry on the cost side of a balance sheet which even in conventional accounting terms was beginning to look alarming.

Concorde was of course an Anglo-French venture: half-Bristol, half-Toulouse, so to speak. Naturally, when the first gleaming white prototype was wheeled out of the hangar at Toulouse Benn was an honoured guest at the ceremony and he was naturally expected to say a few encouraging words. To the general surprise, he announced that, because there had been a failure to agree on the spelling of the name of the aircraft he had resolved it by accepting the French spelling

Concorde. The 'e' on the end, he said, stood for 'Excellence, for England, for Europe and for Entente'. This richly fatuous pronouncement came in for some ribald treatment in the press. The *Guardian* in its Miscellany column was especially sardonic. Under the headline 'A for absurdity' it said that the letter 'e' did indeed stand for many things besides those on Benn's list 'for egomania, ecodysiasts, emigration, effluents, Egypt, elephantiasis, and empty effusions from exasperating envoys, when you come to think of it'.

In truth it was the visionary projects, supplying the epithets for his breathless rhetoric about technology's promised land, which most enthused Benn and which were clearly more to his taste than wrangles with Wrangham or the travails of Greenock's dry dock. He was obviously at his happiest when making pontifical pronouncements on the technological future. In March, for example, he exhorted the Electronic Engineering Association in London to reorganise structurally in order to create powerful UK units to make micro-circuits, and assuring them of government financial support if they would only do as he bade. How agreeable again it must have been in April to lay down the law to 750 delegates from twenty-three countries, when opening the Third Euratom Congress in London, telling them sagely about the fast reactor system being developed at Dounreay and informing them of how the costs of generating power by that method were expected to be 'lower than any other'. How fulfilling to be able to act as well as talk and to be able to allocate, as he did in July, even the piddling sum of £200 000 towards the development of robot assembly units. Still more exciting, in September he was able to unveil the National Research Corporation's £2 million plan to back the tracked Hovertrain principle. Apparently the NRDC had plans to promote world-wide use of high-speed guided land Hovercraft transport systems.

However, in all these cases there was little or nothing that could be called a unifying policy, little evidence of a mind or a will bent to a consistent purpose. Such policy decisions as there were in retrospect look more like the results of chance, the pressure of events reacting with Benn's mercurial enthusiasms. Would a stronger, more determined intelligence insist on a more orderly and determined march into the future? Yes, it seemed that perhaps it would, for Harold Wilson — Mr Purpose in Power himself — took over the supreme direction of the economy in August, and called in Benn and Shore, the two key economic Ministers — Shore had just succeeded Brown as Secretary of State for Economic Affairs. Benn's Ministry in particular, with its responsibility for computers, machine tools and electronics, was going to play a vital part, said a *Guardian* report, in the drive which Mr Wilson was planning for industrial productivity and re-equipment. Could it be that at last the great breakthrough was on its way? Not everybody was ecstatic however: what was the one characteristic which Mr Wilson and his two economic Ministers pledged to revitalise our industry shared? The unkind answer came from the *Daily Mail* — 'the almost total absence of any practical experience of running a business, industrial or commercial, large or small'. A bunch of amateurs in other words; if true, how very wounding to the *amour propre* of this trio who had been primarily identified with Labour's manifesto promise in 1964 to root out amateurism as part of the process of introducing a planned economic expansion based on the exploitation of technology. Wounding or not, this criticism was very much to the point. All three of these politicians were arts degree men, whose skills were almost exclusively words. Wilson, the most important of the three, was amazingly blinkered in practical matters; as Cecil King was to say later in his diaries, Wilson's picture of life was limited by the walls of the House of Commons. His notion of achievement was victory in a vote there. The world outside those walls was of decidedly secondary interest. Action in his eyes was to make a successful speech, to win a debate, to respond to a problem by appointing a Minister or a Royal Commission to produce a report on it this year, next year, sometime, never.

The King view is a little too severe in one respect — reality for Harold Wilson also included the annual Labour party conference, and his dramatic taking-over of personal responsibility for guiding the economy in the summer of 1967 probably owed something to the need to have something to say to that annual gathering of the faithful. Wilson did in fact manage to cobble together a speech which professed to set out the 'proud record of achievement' of the Labour government, during the period which the Tories had labelled 'three years hard Labour'. Things did not look at all promising on the economic front however, with unemployment the worst for thirty years, production stagnant and the balance of payments in seemingly endemic deficit. The most damning comment on Wilson's complacent claims was the Report of the Committee of Enquiry into the Brain Drain, which he himself had appointed and which appeared only five days later, for this showed that in the past six years the number of scientists and engineers leaving Britain annually had doubled to over 6000, most of them in their twenties, and it laid much of the blame on the level of taxation. This was ironic when compared with the speech which Wilson had made at the Scarborough Labour party conference in 1963, where he had maintained strongly that Britain could not let the brain drain go on. 'We are not selling the seed-corn, we are giving it away,' he said and he appealed to scientists not to leave Britain because the new Britain that he and his Ministers were forging needed them.

Benn had naturally been closely concerned with the brain drain as the employer of 10000 scientists and engineers. When the report on the brain drain was discussed on television Benn was asked whether he thought that Britain's scientists left because they needed more money. No, he thought not; it was job satisfaction they were seeking. Apparently the fact that they were the worst paid and more heavily taxed than in any other major country in western Europe had nothing to do with it. In November his over-active mind produced a new alibi and a new scapegoat: it was an American plot. At least, it was at Dounreay, the fast breeder reactor in Caithness, where he was given to understand that twenty-four scientists had answered an advertisement from the Westinghouse Corporation which was prepared to offer them between three and seven times their salaries. Benn exploded with righteous indignation. In an open letter to the scientists he accused the Americans of trying to acquire on the cheap British nuclear technology developed over twenty years at a cost of millions of pounds to the British taxpayer. 'If Westinghouse want good fast reactor technology', he said, 'let them develop their own or buy a licence from us on a proper commercial basis.' Perhaps he was particularly irked with scientists emigrating, arguably at least for economic reasons, because it underlined the folly of the Labour policy document to which he had contributed and which, though secret, had its main provisions revealed in the newspapers in mid-November. It recommended heavy taxes on the 'moderately affluent' — which it appeared to identify as those earning £2000 a year or above. The Dounreay scientists affair finally and rather obscurely collapsed when one of the scientific staff employed there, Murray Cameron, Chairman of Dounreay Staff Association, revealed a few days after Benn's circular letter that the story was a hoax which he himself had perpetrated on the Minister. Apparently, after seeing the Westinghouse advertisements, he had 'planted' the story about numerous applications from Dounreay boffins. His object was to push the Government into expanding work at the fast-breeder instead of running it down. 'Almost no scientists here want to go to America,' he said.

One group of scientists who had no option but to stay where they were were those in the Soviet Union and Benn showed great interest in Anglo-Soviet co-operation throughout his time at Min Tech. New Anglo-Soviet technological agreements were signed in January 1968, though these looked very much like propaganda rituals which followed naturally from the celebrations of the Russian

Revolution's fiftieth anniversary. At a party at the Russian
Embassy in early November 1967 a large posse of Labour
Ministers were present. Asked what they would have done in
October 1917, Lord Chalfont said, 'I would undoubtedly
have been a Bolshevik,' and Kenneth Robinson, Fred Peart,
Anthony Greenwood and Wedgwood Benn felt the same.
Perhaps they were joking, but Benn at least showed willing by
contributing an article on 'Improving Links' to the *Morning
Star* the next day.

Meanwhile, in the economy momentous things were afoot.
Harold Wilson's personal drive for productivity and
efficiency in industry was, like so many of his initiatives, all
words and ink and paper, but this time reality supervened
rather more swiftly than usual. On the 18 November 1967 the
Labour Government announced their decision to devalue the
pound sterling by 14.3 per cent and accompanied that with
other emergency measures, including a higher bank rate,
expenditure cuts and increased taxes. For Wilson above all
others it was a disastrous defeat because he, more than
anyone, had insisted that the pound should not be devalued
and had even banned devaluation as a subject for policy
discussion. Yet, typically, he went on television and made the
tortuous assertion, in a phrase which classically epitomised
his deviousness, that the pound in the man in the street's
pocket would not be devalued. From this moment — piqued
that the economy did not right itself, as it were out of sheer
deference, as soon as he took personal responsibility and
conscious that there was no kudos in failure — Harold
Wilson largely abandoned economic policy, making Roy
Jenkins the new Chancellor of the Exchequer and
bequeathing a secondary, but in socialist terms, still heroic,
role for Benn as arch-interventionist. Anne Scott-James at
least in her *Daily Mail* column saw Benn's promise and
placed him second only to Harold Wilson in her personal
Christmas award for Clown of the Year.

5

INDUSTRIAL
OVERLORD

1968~70

January 1968 marked a new phase in Benn's ministerial career with the publication of the White Paper *Industrial Expansion* since it signalled a decisive shift from the Government's commitment to speeding expansion through the stimulus of a general economic plan to more direct detailed interventionism by Ministers in key sectors and key firms. Under the proposals £100 million would be available to them for a start and £50 million more with the approval of the House of Commons for industrial investment schemes, to support technological advance or to create, sustain or expand production capacity. That was a pretty wide remit, but it was one which especially favoured the extension of Benn's domain. This was partly because the proposals highlighted advanced technology as a sector to be given support and specifically permitted Min Tech to increase advances to the National Research Development Corporation to £500 million. It was also because of the disappearance first of George Brown and subsequently of Harold Wilson himself (who briefly took responsibility for the Department in August 1967) from the DEA scene. Their replacement by the much more junior Peter Shore (more perceptive but less energetic than Benn) gave Britain's Technology Minister the opportunity to become in effect the Government's supreme director of what Harold Wilson had characteristically called 'purposive intervention'.

Benn's own thinking about industry policy at this time, which he later (in a book of his collected speeches) described as 'managerial' was revealed in a Labour meeting in Hampstead in January 1968. As usual, he saw the situation in visionary perspective. After a century of neglect 'the period of construction and reform began in 1964' and industrial reconstruction was 'well under way'. Small fragmented firms were giving way to large undertakings: British Leyland, the world giant of automotive manufacture; Rolls Royce, strengthened by a merger with Bristol Siddeley; shipbuilding, now being organised into a few highly competitive units that could face and beat Japanese competition; and a new electrical giant springing from the merger of GEC and AEI. What an exhilarating prospect this new race of mammoth enterprises seemed to hold out for British industry in the markets of the world! And behind all the modernising, giving national reconstruction its impetus and drive, was a breed of manager who displayed a 'new professionalism and competence of a kind Britain has never known before'. Perhaps Benn saw himself as the epitome, or simply as the voice, of this pushful generation of industrial leaders—professional, competent, possessing natural authority, (merited because it was earned) listening to and learning from them with humility but also, when appropriate, bringing needed state support. Such co-operation between industry and government was in any case, as he saw it, the way of ending stop-go, stagnation and the balance of payments crises which were the bane of British industry.

The message was brimful of hope, and for the moment the auguries seemed to be in his favour. The most immediate application of the policy in the very same month was to the British Leyland/British Motor Holdings merger, over which

The Times enthused in a feature extolling it as the biggest merger in British history but distinguished for the novel manner of its creation. Never before had a private enterprise merger been conceived with such close contact with government, both officials and Ministers, 'right up to Mr Wilson himself'. The new giant, readers were assured, with its plants in Belgium, France and Holland, was well placed to make a major sales assault on the Common Market.

The prospect for export sales was however looking better for a reason unrelated to Benn's growing merger mania, namely the devaluation of the pound in the preceding November, which at a stroke made British goods more competitive in price than for many years. With Callaghan's departure and the arrival of Roy Jenkins as Chancellor of the Exchequer, an orthodox financial policy was followed which at last promised to put the economy on an even keel. It was against this background that we must now consider the work of Benn and the Ministry up to the general election of June 1970.

Under the preceding regime, with George Brown at the Department of Economic Affairs and James Callaghan at the Treasury, the economic government of Britain was an uneasy diarchy with Brown campaigning for growth and Callaghan exercising restraint, so that wits labelled the two ministers 'Mr Stop and Mr Go'. Now the roles might be said to have been passed on with Roy Jenkins organising the 'stop' and Benn supplying whatever was available in the way of 'go'. To judge from the themes of his ceaseless speechifying, Benn's prime concern therefore was as he told Europe's Science Ministers in Paris in March 1968, to close the technological gap between Britain and the United States. The idea that America owed her wealth and power to advanced technology was highly fashionable at this time and owed much to an influential book just published in Britain—*The American Challenge* by the brilliant, if erratic, editor of the French magazine *L'Express,* Jean Jacques Servan-Schreiber. His main contention was that, armed with their superior technology, huge American multinational firms were invading Europe and in effect colonising her industry. Indeed, in fifteen years time, he predicted, the third most powerful force in the world—after the USA and the Soviet Union—would be American industry based in Europe. This argument appealed very much to Harold Wilson, who had made it the centrepiece of his plea for entry into the European Community for which he had made formal application in May 1967. Unless the Europeans got together and pooled their know-how, he warned, they would become technological helots in an Americanised world. The mutual advantage to Britain and the EEC in this context was plain for Britain could bring as her dowry a whole clutch of advanced technological industries—atomic energy, electronics, computers, aircraft and missiles—in which she was substantially ahead of the Community's six existing members. On the other hand, rising development costs meant that Britain would not be able to sustain these industries without the guarantee of a wider market than the domestic market of the UK and in many cases (aerospace for instance) without the assurance of more government support than the British Treasury could supply.

It need not concern us here that the essentially military 'invasion' analogy was inappropriate as a description of the migration of American enterprise to Europe. Far from weakening the European economy, it palpably strengthened it by bringing across the Atlantic not only advanced US technology, but also, and more important, American skill in continental-scale marketing. As a result, more jobs were created and living standards rose. Nor could anyone seriously maintain that European governments were puppets of the multinational companies, since in general these latter sought, often with something approaching obsequiousness, to make themselves acceptable to their host country. Despite this, however wrong-headed the reasoning, the anti-American character of the 1967 approach might have been expected to appeal to President de Gaulle and to persuade him to

Left: A bad line?
The Postmaster General
tries out the new Trim-
phone which 'warbled
like a bird'. *(Sport and
General Press Agency)*

Below: 'Hover Benn'.
The Minister of Tech-
nology examines the 280
mph hovercar. *(Sport and
General Press Agency)*

Top: Industrial overlord. First day at the office after the Technology Ministry had been expanded to include responsibility for the power industries. *(Central Press Photos)*

Bottom: Back-seat driver? The Technology Minister takes off in Concorde 002 with Flight Engineer Brian Watts (right) and test pilot Brian Trubshaw (centre). *(Press Association Photos)*

withdraw the veto which had blocked Britain's entry at the first time of asking. In the event, though, the old General had been unable to see the harm in letting Britain sweat it out a bit longer. Besides, France at that time had burgeoning interests in aerospace, atomic-energy and computers which arguably might progress faster without Britain's entry, while she already enjoyed the advantages of bilateral co-operation with Britain, notably in the case of Concorde. From the French point of view, the Community was in any case working quite satisfactorily, giving full support to French agriculture and effectively letting the French rule the roost through their entente with West Germany in which de Gaulle made the running. So the Wilson application to join the EEC went aground on France's veto in December—another reason for regarding the end of 1967 as the culmination of the first period of the Labour government and the start of something new. Gone now were the hopes both of growth through planning *à la* George Brown and growth assisted or stimulated by Europe. If therefore advanced technology was to provide the means to growth, the sinews would have to be purely national at a time when the state's claims on resources were being retrenched. The implication was that the support Benn gave would have to be very selective.

The difficulty was that the Ministry's programmes were, as the new jargon already had it, 'ongoing' commitments, awkward or impossible to renounce. Concorde, for example, needed another £155 million at the end of February 1968. Benn put a brave face on it; he said, 'For every £1 spent on research and development on a new idea it may take £10 to get it into production and £100 to exploit the market for it. So it pays to be single-minded and not to pursue ideas outside the main business.' That was true up to a point, the point being that it was necessary to make the right choice in the first place. There was no virtue in single-mindedly backing losers. As George Gale wisely and wittily put it in the *Daily Mirror* as he reflected on the further huge subsidies being lavished on the supersonic aircraft being built in Benn's constituency,

'We'd do far better if he used our cash to buy a few old masters, some stamps and tons of Georgian silver'. By October, the cost of Concorde had soared by a further £50 million because of delays, inflation and wage increases on the French half of the work. The research and development bill had by this time reached £700 million—five times the original estimate. By December Benn was announcing that there had been 'some stoppage in the production schedules'. In January 1969 he was telling the House of Commons that the overall bill (shared between Britain and France) could rise to £1000 million and a few days later he was obliged to deny the rumour that Concorde would be scrapped, at the same time making the indignant plea that people should stop knocking it. Even he however had little encouragement to offer when the best answer he could give in reply to a question on 21 May from John Biffen about whether he expected to recoup a substantial part of the costs, was that it would depend on orders, but that he hoped to get back about one third of the money. With winners like that the promised growth through selective technological stimulus would have to wait a long time.

The main point of detailing this phase of the Concorde's development is to show how out of control it appeared to be. Benn's Ministry, far from being master of its fate, was more like an investor locked into a partly-paid share and never sure when the next call for funds would come. What the rhetoric of Benn's speeches might represent as a deliberate exercise in picking what looked like a sure thing and then single-mindedly sticking to it through thick and thin was in fact a case of being dragged helplessly in the wake of a project which had acquired a momentum of its own. And despite the mounting cost—at any particular moment, whatever the momentary uproar whenever the cost jumped, however much further ahead of the estimate—the easiest thing for the Minister responsible to do was to soldier on, throwing good money after bad, since this exacted a much lower political cost than the upheaval of cancellation. (In Benn's case, because Concorde was made in Bristol, the penalty could well have been his parliamentary seat.)

The same impression of a Ministry progressively losing control applied in the case of the Upper Clyde Shipbuilders. The theory (that big organisations are best) which gave birth to that ill-fated shipbuilding consortium was that of the Geddes report on Shipbuilding of March 1966. The hope was that a merger of five ship yards—Charles Connell, John Brown, Alexander Stephen, Fairfields and Yarrow—would make a larger, commercially more viable unit, but even before it started trading in February 1968, the unions had managed to foil the central proposal of the working party: that the labour force should be reduced from 13 000 to 7 500. Instead UCS was able to start only after guaranteeing employment for all the workers for two years. Thereafter it was inevitable that it would need rescuing time after time. By May 1969 the company was facing liquidation and demanded aid of £12 million. Benn appeared in Glasgow, describing his visit as the 'moment of truth', but the main truth was that the combine had made heavy losses on deliberately (and, as it turned out, ruinously) low tenders made with the intention of keeping the workload full. At this stage, Benn may well have been determined to read the riot act and point out, as he told the House of Commons, that there was no safety net beneath any firm or industry in this country. Unfortunately there was one kind of pressure which it was impossible for him to resist.

During the Whitsun recess one of Glasgow's Labour MPs died and the prospect of fighting a by-election in the city after UCS had closed down was more than Willie Ross, the Secretary of State for Scotland or his cabinet colleagues could face. So Benn returned to Glasgow and handed out £9 million, leaving it to his assistant Gerry Fowler to spell out the message in the House of Commons that this was the Government's limit, 'not least because it would mean that UCS was subsidised against other British competition as well as against foreign competition'. That should have been the end of the matter in 1969 at least. Yet lo and behold, on the

11 December, Benn appeared in the House of Commons to announce that UCS was to have a further £7 million: the 'wider social and economic considerations' to which he referred in his speech had evidently been too much for him. The position had been neatly put earlier at a Scottish Nationalist conference, which coincided with one of the UCS crises, by a speaker from the floor, who said, 'We hear that Mr Benn proposes to come to Glasgow himself. We say to him "Don't bother to come to Glasgow—just send us the money." '. It was not as if all the subsidies ever achieved the main aim of preserving jobs in shipbuilding since direct subsidy to ailing yards had helped to raise the wage costs of those that were still competitive. *The Economist* on the 18 April 1970 summed up thus: '. . . the net result of the Government's largesse has been to create a situation in which two giant yards with full order books find themselves facing staggering losses, and perhaps bankruptcy and closure in the middle of a world shipbuilding boom without precedent'. Of course the position could only worsen once the boom collapsed.

One of the more colourful episodes in the history of UCS was its building of the QE2. This was delivered late, partly because of deliberate delays by the workers aimed at boosting overtime payments. Another factor was the sensational amount of pilferage. One Glasgow story had it that the carpets carried up one gangway during completion were immediately taken away down another to be sold—no doubt for the benefit of some practically-minded egalitarians who asked themselves why the workers should not have a slice of the £24 million subsidy for this prestige ship. When the QE2 went on its trial, the engine broke down, which evoked a certain amount of ribaldry in the media. Benn became rather shirty over the criticisms levelled at the slow completion time of the ship (on the theory presumably that only fellow-toilers like himself were entitled to allude to the imperfections of any members of the working class). He also called for a 'respectful silence' for the engineers who were trying to sort out the turbines. This was rather like a Victorian vicar protesting 'Is nothing sacred?'. The comparison has a certain pertinence because Benn does seem to have certain subjects which he regards with something approaching religious awe, such as the working class or technology or (this is to anticipate) the democratic process, and about which he considers jokes to be in bad taste. It was no doubt a Freudian slip when he put forward a plan in April 1969 for what he called 'Cathedrals of Technology' — i.e. municipal showcases for modern technical marvels, where indeed the people could and worship.

However that may be, the above examples show that picking winners is not a piece of cake, especially for a politician under pressure from lobbies. Though he may know that a particular group or interest is merely seeking his co-operation to protect it against competition, he also knows that the workers concerned have votes, and the temptation is to present what is essentially a surrender to a vocal section of the electorate as a step towards a glittering technological future. It is of course possible that it may be both. There may conceivably be cases where the Minister may see better than the investing community. Benn could make a good case out for himself for his backing of International Computers Limited with loans, grants, development and production contracts (indeed, creating it by merging International Computers and Tabulators and English Electronic Computers). At least, in this case, he was putting money behind an expanding industry with dazzling growth potential and the amounts involved were not very large when compared with what Concorde guzzled up — £17 million for instance to promote the ICT merger. This meant that Britain's computer industry, unlike most of those abroad (outside the United States), had a national firm in a commanding position in the domestic market, which meant that the American giant, International Business Machines, did not acquire three-quarters of the sales as happened in many other comparable countries. This looks like a definite gain, but is it? It is after all more important for the growth of the economy to *use* computers than to *make* them, and it is possible that the failure of Britain to maintain her lead in Europe of the early sixties in the quantity of computer power installed was due to protecting British computer manufactur and making a sales drive by IBM less attractive in Britain than for instance in West Germany.

As any punter could have told Benn, even betting on what appears to be a certainty does not always pay; the best horse can miss its footing. A case in point was the Rolls Royce RB-211 jet engine. (A contract for the installation of this engine in the Lockheed 10-11 airbus was won by Rolls Royce at the end of March 1968. There was only one snag—the company needed government finance to the tune of seventy per cent of development costs. Benn made a snap decision and committed £47.1 million in very quick time. It was a large sum, but to an amateur in investment matters like Benn, it must have looked like investing in success. The *Sun* typified the rapture with which the press greeted what was undoubtedly a brilliant sales achievement against foreign competition with its headline 'Rolls Hit the Jackpot'. In the event, costs escalated and by the end of 1969 the Industrial Re-organisation Corporation was itching to give the company an unsecured loan of £20 million. It was only after Benn had left his ministerial post that it was revealed how disastrous in inflationary times a fixed price contract for a product, on which the full development costs were unknown, could actually turn out to be.

Many of the decisions confronting Benn were really more to do with investment than technology, not that he knew a great deal about technology either, but why should he — especially if he was apt (as we have seen) to ignore the views of his industrial advisers — know better than the stock market? Thus against the advice of the Ministry working party, he launched a £2 500 000 scheme for insuring against losses on stockpiled production of machine tools but by April, only one firm — Staveley, the scheme's original advocate — took it up. Perhaps he was lucky that no others did. The theory of smoothing out fluctuations in demand by guaranteeing stocks of products unsold is obvious enough. Yet, as the history of commodity buffer-stock schemes bears witness, it is fraught with dangers, the chief one being that what is thought to be a fluctuation of demand within an overall trend may in the event prove to be a change of trend. Then the buffer stock becomes a de-stabilising factor, and there is no faster way of losing money than gambling against the trend.

Many of Benn's decisions about where to plunge with the taxpayers' money were indeed not the result of any grand strategy or consistent industrial philosophy but more the result of circumstance and whim, of the 'it seemed like a good idea at the time' syndrome. It is nevertheless worth considering whether there is some retrospective justification, say because the policy was better than the predictions, or because his actions were wiser than he knew. Is there anything in the general theory that lavish support of high technology can give the economy a stimulus it cannot obtain anywhere else? Professor Jewkes has suggested (in *'Government and High Technology'* IEA, 1972) that 'High technology' is not the same as 'advanced' but merely 'high cost' technology which governments tend to go for because nobody else can afford it. (It may, of course, yield a political return to governments even if it is unprofitable commercially, because it associates the rulers with glamorous and exciting technical achievements — the moonshot being an example.) The cause, says Jewkes, is fear on the part of modern industrial countries with high living standards that they will be overtaken by the poorer nations. Besides, there are many politicians who are simply dazzled by the technical devices which make the newspaper headlines; as Lord Beeching said, 'I think that (the British government) has wasted an enormous amount of money on things justified by the pursuit of advanced technology — an almost childlike desire to play with toys'. In some cases (certainly Benn's) high technology is 'the last refuge of the enthusiastic nationalist'. This is often associated with the delusion that big organisations are the most efficient and that there is a pronounced trend towards industrial concentration. Benn himself said in *The Times* 'Giant corporations hold the future of world's high technology in their hands'. This, even at that time, was a hoary old superstition with no statistical justification, as Professor Jewkes has shown in another IEA publication in 1977: *Delusions of Dominance.* In fact the industrial structure has been remarkably stable all over the western world for a generation and if we go back to the turn of the century the amount of concentration in industry has probably declined. Nor is bigness a guarantee of efficiency and profitability; it is often the reverse. In *The Times 1 000 Companies,* the return on capital employed seems to improve as the size of business decreases. (See *Mergers, Takeovers and the Structure of Industry,* IEA, 1973.)

It is a sad, but perhaps instructive, fact that many on the Left of the Labour party feel some extraordinary compulsion to make their number with the Soviet Union and, at the risk of whatever intellectual contortions, attempt to incorporate into the framework of their professed compassion some personal *modus vivendi* with that horrendous regime. Benn was no exception; as Minister of Technology his opportunity was perhaps better than that of most of his colleagues because his own eagerness for personal *détente* was matched by an equivalent urge on the Soviet side to make what use it could of British expertise. Thus, in mid May 1969 he visited Russia at the invitation of his opposite number, Mr Kirilin, who had been to Britain on previous official junkets and had met Benn then. Benn, as usual, took note only of what interested him (at least that is the charitable interpretation), since he did not so much as raise a peep about Gerald Brooke, a British citizen who had languished for four years in Soviet jails. As a *Daily Telegraph* editorial pointedly put it, 'Mr Wedgwood Been underlined the spinelessness of the British attitude by not once raising the case'. It made it slightly worse that Benn was also the first British Minister to visit Moscow since Soviet troops entered Czechoslovakia the previous August. It all contributed to the Kremlin's impression that we did not care what they did. While in Russia he lectured them on the damage which imperialism had done to the British economy — quoting Marx in the course of his speech — in that it had diverted Britain from the task of industrial modernisation and ultimately burdened the economy with heavy defence expenditure. It was ingenious, but rested on the rather strange assumption that the Russian ruling class would see the analogy with their empire today and would mend their ways because they were consumer democrats at heart. Benn returned to Britain with the message that the Russians were keen to acquire British goods. No doubt they were, but the consistent surplus they ran on their trade with Britain suggests that they did not like paying for them or preferred to acquire them on tick which, as long as there were people like Benn and Wilson in charge, must have seemed a reasonable possibility.

Thus far we have been concerned with Wedg Benn of Min Tech, who, on his own admission, was to start with at least rather managerial in his outlook. That is why it is necessary to pay particular attention to an episode in 1968 which either gave birth to or, more likely, precipitated a transformation of the way he saw the world and placed him, as he saw it, no longer in the political establishment, but firmly among the people. The dramatic events in Paris in May 1968, when the students went on strike, occupied the Sorbonne and set in train events leading to de Gaulle's downfall, led Benn to rise like an Old Testament prophet and launch into a wild harangue to the Welsh Council of Labour, who, as it happened, were in a suitably disturbed state of mind to receive it because of an explosion which had taken place the night before at the Welsh Office in Cardiff. His theme was that — however unwelcome — radical reform would have to come because if not, 'discontent, expressing itself in despairing apathy of violent protest, could engulf us all in bloodshed. It is no good saying it could never happen here. It could.' He went on to say that it was necessary for 'popular democracy' to replace the existing parliamentary system since technology (for Benn, the villain or hero of every piece) was outdating our institutions, his main reform being the use of referenda to give the people more say in policy making. It was actually a rather turgid speech, but its coverage in the press could not have disappointed him. However, as many hastened to point out, the referendum — a prominent feature of de Gaulle's style of government — was a strange institution to borrow from France as a means of avoiding in Britain the violence which was occurring there. The mention of bloodshed also reminded some of Enoch Powell's earlier speech about immigration, the main objection to which had been its extravagant language, notably the phrase in which Powell pictured the future as like Rome when the Tiber flowed with much blood.

There were certainly discontents galore in Britain at the time Benn spoke, but these sprang not from anything so abstract as the obsolete character of parliamentary government, but from more mundane and material causes: soaring prices, heavy unemployment, a stagnant economy and what the public opinion polls showed to be an extremely unpopular government which could not be constitutionally removed for another two or three years. Richard Crossman wrote contemptuously in his diary of Benn's speech, saying that 'his one concrete suggestion' for improving British democracy was the adoption of 'an electronic referendum'. But, he continued, 'As Duncan Sandys once pointed out, a referendum on capital punishment, homosexuality, prices and incomes, or Rhodesia would be quite sure to bring a defeat of the Government. The trouble with Wedgy is that his presentation is brilliant but what he says is normally second-rate and sometimes disastrously stupid.' This was indeed one of the occasions when the presentation was alpha and the content gamma minus. Crossman might have added that anybody on Labour's National Executive, especially if placed there by the card vote of the union bosses, was in no position to pontificate about democracy. Even so, it seems right to date to the exciting stimulus in 1968 of the French example a definite shift in Benn's outlook, because it was from this time onwards that he unfailingly displayed an eager-beaver concern with participatory democracy. It was considered to be largely at his behest that a document called *Industrial Democracy,* providing for workers' (meaning union) representation on the boards of their firms, was endorsed by Labour's National Executive that July as part of the agenda for party's national conference at Blackpool in October. (Ironically it was reported the following day that metrication, for which Benn was responsible, was to be brought into force in Britain by 1975—not much participation there for all its dressing up with an advisory board said to represent everybody, since the public opinion was patently overwhelmed by vested interests.

Benn's urge to communicate, almost regardless of the communication's content, was as we have seen compulsive, and it was shortly after the Labour party conference of 1968 that he made what was surely his most celebrated, and also his most inept, pronouncement on the communications industry. In a speech to the Bristol Labour party he launched a furious assault on the BBC which he accused of comment-coloured news, over-used instant pundits, triviality, and politician-baiting which encouraged contempt for those in public life. He then warned that 'broadcasting is really too important to be left to the broadcasters'. Some way had to be found, he said, of establishing representative broadcasting in place of the paternalism of 'the constitutional monarchs who reside in Broadcasting House'. In the light of these last remarks it seemed rather fatuous for him to say at the same time that he was not proposing government control of the mass media. Whatever else it was, or was not, the speech was bound to be taken as an attack on the Corporation's independence especially as, in pointing to what was needed, Benn had used the ominous phrase 'firm framework of public service control'. He was understood, surely rightly, to be wishing to deny the BBC the editorial function performed by newspapers, and to be saying in effect that anyone could do a good broadcast if he put his mind to it. Surely here was the man who was constantly sniping at the amateurism in British business, blandly denying the value of professionalism in a sphere where the meanest intelligence could see it was needed—namely in the organisation and presentation of programmes where the costs of production are high and time, being limited, is money.

In fact Benn's criticism of the BBC ranged too wide, as he was really blaming it for the failures in communication by a wide variety of institutions, including parliament, the churches, the scientific community and the unions; moreover, he was urging that the channels be opened up to representatives of these and other organised interests to put over their message in their own way. Yet the result could only be unexampled tedium, rather like the stuff being dished out on the other side of the Iron Curtain, or a widening of the principle of the party political broadcast. In any case, there was universal alarm. Ray Gunter, who had earlier in the year resigned from the Cabinet, asked whether Benn had spoken with or without the knowledge of his colleagues and asked why ITV had not been included in the indictment. What he was getting at was whether Benn, with his chief's support, was carrying on Harold Wilson's old vendetta against the BBC. Gunter's first guess was apparently nearer the mark. A few days later the Prime Minister made a ruling that controversial speeches by members of the Cabinet should be cleared with him beforehand. Benn at the same time complained that his remarks had been distorted (even though he was very fully reported). His 'broadcasting is too important to be left to the broadcasters' he said was taken out of context 'like accusing a Chartist of wanting to go back to the Divine Right of Kings'—an impressively obscure argument which contributed nothing towards healing the breach with the professionals concerned in making BBC programmes, who felt they had been traduced.

Still Benn was not to be put down: a fortnight later, speaking about how more and more people were banding together to get things done outside the party system, he said that the Labour party had a lot to learn from political action groups like Black Power — a classic bit of headline stealing. Did they but know it, the Black Power boys could probably have learnt a lot from Benn.

Such escapades might annoy his colleagues, as the Crossman diaries indicate, but did not stop the steady advancement of Benn's career. Harold Wilson regarded him as a good Minister, even if he did talk nonsense a good deal of the time and by Wilson's criteria, which placed a higher value on image-building and the projection of caring and competence than on actually getting things done, a good Minister he certainly was. Even more to the point, Benn saw eye-to-eye with his leader on a great many things, and had the same sci-fi interest in technology, the same single-minded dedication to politics and correspondingly narrow outlook on life. No matter that he made no secret of his ambition to go to the top, for Wilson did not see in him a serious threat to himself, especially as he was of an age not to be in too great a hurry. The very openness of his ambition indeed was almost endearing: what could have been more transparent than the scheme put up in July 1968 by Jeremy Bray (parliamentary secretary in Benn's Ministry) for making the General Secretary of the Labour party an automatic member of the Labour Cabinet? It was obvious that the person Bray had in mind for this job was his ministerial boss, who when Labour was in office would rank second only to the Prime Minister himself and rank equally with the leader when the party was in opposition. The proposal came and went. Briefly it was a talking point and then it disappeared to be heard of no more. Wilson valued Benn as a publicist. He might be too leftist for the middle ground, but he compensated for his provocative radicalism with his inspirational qualities, and with his readiness with ideas, for example his interesting proposal for the 1968 conference that Labour should publicly confess their past mistakes. For confession, apart from being good for the soul, also makes parties look human. Again, though he might be dotty about electric cars and electronic referenda, at least he made politics interesting, and nothing was, or is, more fatal to democratic politics than boredom. Perhaps most important of all, considering how conspiracy conscious Wilson was, Benn went out of his way more than once to call for unity under the party's leader.

All these factors no doubt contributed to Wilson's decision, when reconstructing his government in October 1969, to give one of the two super Ministries which he created out of a number of lesser ones, to Benn, characteristically giving the other one to Crosland in an attempt to keep the balance of Left and Right. The Ministry of Technology was expanded to include, in addition to its old responsibilites: the coal and fuel responsibilities of the Ministry of Power and such industries as textiles and paper which had formerly come under the Board of Trade. It also gobbled up the DEA's responsibility for regional industrial development, most of the little Neddies and the Industrial Reorganisation Corporation. Sir Keith Joseph, the opposition spokesman, commented that 'This vast amorphous jellyfish of a department will be flabby and inert because it has been given too much to do'.

But Benn, however busy, was interested primarily in the promised land of socialism and, as 1970 went by, in the prospect of an election which would make feasible a further giant step down the socialist road. Suddenly the opinion polls which had consistently favoured the Tories started moving back towards Labour. Roy Jenkins's orthodox financial policy was, amazingly enough, starting to pay off. Wilson's personal standing improved, while that of Heath crumbled. All the evidence suggests that it was these polls which persuaded Wilson to take the chance in June. True to his enthusiastic nature, Benn flung himself into the fight, but his talent for publicity this time led him astray. Addressing 200 left-wing students in London on 3 June he made a bitter attack on Enoch Powell for his 'racism', saying that the flag hoisted over Wolverhampton 'was beginning to look like the one that fluttered over Dachau and Belsen'. Powell replied with dignity at a meeting at Southwick as follows: 'All that I will say is that in 1939 I voluntarily returned from Australia to this country to serve as a private soldier in the war against Germany and Nazism. I am the same man today.' Benn had committed a fatal error, since Powell, who had been expelled from the Shadow Cabinet by Heath and had ever since posed a threat to Tory unity, was made to appear by Benn's attack at one with his party. It was no small, if negative, achievement by Benn that he actually provoked Heath into a defence of Powell. All the same, the public opinion polls had been showing Labour well ahead, except for the Harris Poll on the day of the count, which in an inspired moment Humphrey Taylor, the poll's managing director, adjusted for differential abstention and put the Tories on top. The poll actually took place on Waterloo day and it decided that among other things, Benn's Ministerial empire was no more.

6

FRENZY IN OPPOSITION

1970~2

For the whole Labour party the 1970 election defeat was a shock, and for no-one more than Harold Wilson, who, though he protested that he took no notice of public opinion polls, actually studied them keenly and, instant pragmatist that he was, based much of his policy on them. Imagine then how shattering it must have been, after a series of polls putting his party well in front and with National Opinion Poll actually giving a Labour lead of 12.4 per cent at the end of the second week of the campaign, that in the end he still managed to snatch defeat from the jaws of victory!

Benn probably had not had much time to think about this. He revelled in elections and on the eve of poll he had had six meetings in his constituency. (It was also, as it happened, his twenty-first wedding anniversary, but, as his wife Caroline said, 'I think we shall have to wait for our twenty-second anniversary for a relaxed celebration'.) All the effort must have seemed rather wasted when the result was announced because the swing in Bristol North East to the Conservatives was 6.1% — well above the national average of 4.7% — but still leaving Benn with what looked the comfortable majority of 10.8 per cent, though the fact that two other Bristol seats in the north-east and north-west of the city were lost to the Conservatives must have looked ominous. Still the thing is, as all seasoned campaigners know, to put on the best face you can and Benn issued a statement saying that there must be no despair and insisting that 'History will be more generous to our Labour government than the results suggest'.

Meanwhile, what was to happen to yesterday's men and women, tipped out of their ministries, their salaries and official cars suddenly forfeit? Barbara Castle said she would take up cooking again. Dick Crossman, lucky chap, was off to edit the *New Statesman*. Benn told *The Observer,* 'I've always regarded Parliament as a full-time job. My profession is journalism, so I shall write as well. I wouldn't consider any other work. I've had no offers.' In fact he was one of the comparative minority on the Labour side (or any side) who were not forced by material circumstances to work at all. It was indeed the independence which his capitalist situation conferred which allowed him, like Marx's friend, Friedrich Engels, the luxury of devoting his life to encompassing the destruction of the capitalist system. He did however return to doing some journalism in the *New Statesman* and he was soon writing there in disparagement of his successors at Min Tech.

A month later in the poll which the Labour Parliamentary party annually holds to decide who shall be in the Shadow Cabinet, Benn came well up, taking fifth place out of the chosen twelve. A few days after the poll Benn went as usual to address the Durham Miners at their annual Gala, when he made a perhaps predictable call for better 'communications' (already an established 'in' word) between unions and the public. He said that big business spent millions of pounds on advertising, propaganda and public relations, and to win support the unions must do the same.

It was at this juncture that Benn found time to produce a pamphlet for the Fabian Society called *The New Politics, A Socialist Reconnaissance.* This was a wide ranging statement of his general approach to politics which, if not very sprightly, had the merit that it brought together the themes to which he has subsequently returned time and again. The ideas were trendy rather than original, but as a formulation of Benn's populism it was very useful if only as a guide to how in any given situation he was likely to react. The pamphlet started by observing the general disenchantment with British politics which it attributed to the mistaken belief of the parties that what people cared about was economic management. In fact, he thought that people were more concerned that, as the power of technology increased, they would have less and less say over their lives since technology had made the world more complicated, made us more dependant on others, and fostered big industry and big government both nationally and internationally. To make the conflict worse we had a new kind of citizen, better off, better educated, less deferential and more capable of dislocating the system than in the past. The result had been a great growth of protest and community action. People wanted more say in decisions affecting them, the demand was ever more insistent. We needed frequent referenda and workers' control; authoritarianism in government or industry was out-dated; secrecy which protected incompetence and privilege had to be renounced in favour of open government. The mass media had to be democratised to give the people direct access to programmes and print. Education had to be comprehensive, not elitist, and the idolatry of examinations abandoned. The state needed to be comprehensive too, allocating all resources and taking care of everybody. Meanwhile, at all levels there was to be constant discussion which called for a new form of leadership, consultative as opposed to autocratic, the archetypal leader being Moses, the ten commandments presumably being an early form of O and M report. (This was of course long before Moses Callaghan took over as Prime Minister.)

This pamphlet undoubtedly contained genuine insights into modern political dilemmas, but it was also undermined by some fallacious and dubious assumptions. For a start, why did he believe that the undoubted disenchantment with politics was due to the politicians' obsession with economic issues? It would be more true to say of Britain at least that people *were* mainly worried about the bread and butter questions on which the politicians had concentrated, and that frustration arose because it was in this very area that politicians had so dismally failed. What classically illustrates that failure is the fact that, whereas the British standard of living before the Second World War was double that of Western Germany, now it is only half. Nor was it obvious that people were in the main alienated or even bewildered by technology (which, in most ways, was making life more bearable by keeping people better fed, clothed and housed and had reduced enormously the burden of human toil. Besides, the idea of increasing economic concentration was merely a Marxist myth, for there has been very little change in the size distribution in manufacturing concerns (let alone service organisations) in the last half century; nor was the centralised bureaucratic state a necessary result of advanced technology — historically it has more often been an indication of political and economic backwardness, being a notable feature of for instance the seedier days of imperial Spain or the Ottoman Empire.

Of people's desire for more say over their lives, the only evidence of this was perhaps the growth of protest, but this could very plausibly be attributed to the extension of socialism and union tyranny which had increased the amount of external coercion to which people were subject. They may indeed have felt a loss of power over their own destinies, but this was perhaps because of what Walt Whitman called the 'never ending insolence of elected men' and the mounting scale of official interference in their lives. As far as the new citizen was concerned, the astonishing thing was surely that there should have been any dispute about whether he was or was not worse educated than his forbears fifty years ago, despite the billions spent on schools and universities.

Discontent in industry seemed to be rife (though not perhaps rifer than in the two decades preceding the Great War), but this was surely due in great part to inflation, the ultimate cause of which was excessive state spending. In any case, current discontents did not necessarily imply a desire for more participation in government — the obligation to participate in discussions, political education and confessions being one of the more trying characteristics of the world's nastier regimes, an example being post-revolutionary Cambodia. People might on the contrary want to be left alone. In practice the 'people having their say' is all too often just a matter of giving undue power to unrepresentative pressure groups, a particular danger of Benn's scheme for giving the people access to the media. With regard to referenda, it is suspicious how selective is the enthusiasm of Benn and his friends for using this instrument to test the popular will since they have never got within miles of proposing that referenda should be used to determine the popular will on hanging, homosexual law reform or reductions in taxation, on which the Bennite Left would lose hands down. Fundamentally, the Benn idea was that the General Will should embrace and permeate all activities. He did not seem to realise the totalitarian implications of this view or the contradiction involved in his denunciation of bureaucracy (which, with so much power at the centre, would be inevitable). He seems also quite deaf to the claims of the free market as a method of popular participation, yielding satisfaction at the same time as giving power to the consumer. Perhaps because in his own personal life he has been able to take them for granted, he does not appear either to understand the importance of property rights — which he would quite happily dispense with as part of his exercise in workers' control. Just how without such an institution it would be possible to guarantee enough people who were economically independent of government to resist the central authority, he did not explain. Admittedly, property rights may be vested in the workers in the form of say, a plant collective, but the Yugoslav example is hardly encouraging.

Even if there are many objections to Benn's views (not the least being that they often reflect passing enthusiasms) they seem to be held genuinely enough, and there is nothing like conviction, even if mistaken, for getting politics on the move and few things more likely to mark a man out from his fellows in these pragmatic times. In any event, Benn had an opportunity to convert one of his hobby horses, the referendum, into a ready-made campaign for a British referendum on Common Market membership, launched less than a fortnight after the pamphlet's publication. He began the campaign by the time-honoured method of addressing his constituents in a 4500-word letter. Essentially his case was that entering Europe was an 'irreversible decision which would transfer certain sovereign powers now exercised by the British parliament to the European Economic Community. Parliament would then be obliged to carry through those changes in its law that were necessary to implement Community policy and the courts would have to uphold and enforce community law in Britain. If people are not to participate in this decision no-one will ever take participation seriously again.'

At the annual conference at the end of September Benn was in full spate once more, warning, or at least broadly hinting, that a future Labour government would not pay compensation in the case of renationalisation of firms. When the proposal came before Labour's National Executive the following January, it was postponed and in effect killed off, though nobody — including Roy Jenkins — objected to the principle.

Benn's appointment as Chairman of the Labour party's publicity committee in November gave him an ideal platform for putting across his ideas about participatroy politics. He was especially anxious that communication between the leadership and the rank and file should be improved. This involved among other things being more open with information for the party workers about the doings of the party Executive and its committees — though it looks rather like a politician's fond fancy to imagine that the ordinary party worker would be all that interested in what is for the most part mundane, routine business. However, to mark the new approach, the Director of Publicity at Transport House (Mrs Penny Clark) was renamed Director of Information. Benn was also anxious to involve the constituency workers in policy formation and he put up to the Executive the suggestion that as a start the local parties should be asked to identify those policies which required rethinking. A couple of months later he was urging the National Executive in a special paper to offer 'consultative status' to pressure groups like the Child Poverty Action Group, Shelter, the Disablement Income Group, World Poverty Action (and no doubt Bachelor Mums) — 6000 bodies altogether. This he argued was in imitation of the United Nations, which gave to non-governmental organisations special privileges of access to documents etc. and even opportunity to speak at UN conferences. The snag with this idea was that the United Nations is not a potential government (as a political party is) so it can encourage minority pressure groups in the knowledge that it will never be obliged to implement their recommendations. In contrast, if a party gives pressure groups special access to the policy makers, it is in danger of making itself the tool of unrepresentative minorities. Organisationally too it is a recipe for chaos, inevitably putting the party officials at the beck and call of lobbying groups — 'consultative status' means that there must be somebody to consult with on a regular basis. The likely result is that a political party adopting the Benn approach of 'let 'em all come' will be deluged with liaison committees, special connections and little fiefdoms. In fact it could finish up with a hierarchical shambles like the Holy Roman Empire, and from a practical political point of view just as ineffective.

Benn had, as usual, been quick to seize upon ideas which happened to be floating around, and the concept of community politics had already been going the rounds for some years. It was the basis of a rather quaint exercise indulged in by the Conservative Central Office over three years before and labelled 'Project 67' — and by sceptics, rightly as it turned out, 'Reject 68'. This exercise was aimed at making the constituency committees more representative of the voters — not necessarily a good idea. For one thing, the activists of all parties always include an inordinately high proportion of the middle class, and it would be unrealistic to seek to change this radically because presumably it reflects the fact of life that political activity within political parties is a disproportionately bourgeois activity like golf. Perhaps the most important quality in a political party is its acceptability and a part of that may be the consistency with which it conforms to the stereotype it has acquired in the eyes of the public.

Much the best idea Benn had as Chairman of Labour's publicity committee was the launching of a Labour Party weekly paper. This was in the outcome quite a sensible venture and for a time led to sales at newsagents, and it was copied by the Conservative in their *Monthly News*. But, again typically of Benn, there was a lack of follow-through. Neither party has so far understood how to use publications to bolster membership activity because both party organisations are dominated by their agents. In fact a good direct publications list can be used to advertise meetings and functions all over the country far more effectively than the extremely thin constituency agents' network, especially when party activists' enthusiasm is wasting away. The organisation to learn this lesson — the National Association for Freedom — had not yet been born, but later on its newspaper *The Free Nation* combined with well publicised legal actions on behalf of the cause, like Grunwick, was to push membership and the sales of its newspaper over the 40 000 mark, while its meetings even in the provinces often topped the 1000 mark.

In any event, it was questionable whether Benn's urgent desire to get moving on the policy-making front, however participatory the method of its formulation, was shared by

Harold Wilson and others among Labour's ruling junta. Anthony Crosland was at this time strongly of the opinion that elaborate new policies were unnecessary; indeed he thought that all the participation stuff was a dangerous distraction. In opposition, theories are usually more rewarding than detailed policies because detail always gives hostages to fortune. The Labour party in particular is liable to arouse normally unpolitical businessmen from their slumbers and alert them to the need to defend themselves from nationalisation and confiscatory taxes. Clearly there is something to be said for vagueness. Labour's success in 1964 had owed something to the spadework put in by Harold Wilson and others at boardroom lunches in assuaging the fears of stockbrokers and industrialists by generally fudging issues with a blanket of optimism, modernisation chatter and assurances that they had nothing to fear from a Labour government, but much to gain from an end to stop-go. If Benn's constituency cohorts got their way, or at any rate their say, any such buttering-up of the business community would be rendered unproductive.

Benn's view that you might as well be frank about what you stand for was more appealing, and shrewder than it looked. When it comes to voting, people are rarely swayed so much by ideology as by rather more mundane considerations, such as whether their living conditions are improving or worsening. So, if people do not actually read the fine print in the manifesto and do not care either, perhaps it is best to make sure that the fine print does contain all the things you really intend to do because this makes it possible to justify your actions at a later stage by saying that that was policy which the people approved when they voted. That could at least be the reason why, when his colleagues were still licking their wounds and wondering what had gone wrong that they should find themselves out of office, that Benn in his speeches was moving still further leftwards. Thus, shortly before Christmas 1970 he strayed into the educational field and announced his hostility to the examination system.

'From the age that a child enters primary school to the day of his death, he is judged, tested, selected, graded, employed and promoted according to his paper qualifications.' No doubt there was something in this lament, but Benn might also have reflected that it is above all the characteristic of bureaucracies to make undue fuss about paper qualifications. Besides, as Dr Rhodes Boyson pointed out at the time, 'Who would want to go to a doctor whose skill has never been examined and who, with no fear of future failure, had never attended lectures?'.

It all looked as if Benn was riding high and was adding to his stature within the party by using his important position as Chairman of its publicity committee to project himself all over the country as the man of the future, when he started to get caught up with some of the embarrassments bequeathed by the past. Many in the Labour party had had an uneasy felling that Benn's antics in the 1970 election, though they caught the headlines, may have done more harm than good to their cause. In February 1971, this widespread hunch received startling confirmation from the Harris Poll which showed that Benn's attack on Enoch Powell during the campaign was 'the biggest single blunder of the campaign, because it rallied working class support to Powell'. There were also the disappointing results of the brave, if not very sensible, hopes or receptacles of them, into which he had plunged with so much taxpayers' money while in office. The bankruptcy of Rolls Royce in February 1971 may not have been Edward Heath's finest hour, especially in view of his subsequent conversion to, and enthusiasm for, state direction and financial support for ailing firms, but, as the Rolls Royce story unfolded, it did not do much good to Benn's reputation either, especially considering how vain Benn had been about the moment when he took the big decision to back Rolls's RB-211 engine. Rolls directors came to him one evening in March 1968, saying they must have a pledge of £20 million within five and a half hours to sew up the deal with Lockheed before the board of that company met in New York. Later

Benn described proudly how he had seen similar situations on television in *The Power Game* or *The Planemakers* when governments were frightfully slow to make big decisions. So, in this rather romantic frame of mind Benn duly took the plunge, not with the £20 million but a bridging loan of £9 million, which rose to £47 million once Rolls Royce gained the contract. In fact Rolls Royce had been so keen to clinch the deal that they offered a foolishly low price and failed to safeguard themselves against inflation. In the event, the company was unable to deliver and faced a total potential liability of £150 million.

Admittedly, Benn was not the only politician to be bamboozled by the Lockheed contract; indeed, there was general applause for his bold actions at the time, but the whole episode was a revealing illustration of how ill-suited is the populist political mentality to making decisions about investing money. The politician's aim is not so much to maximise profit as to harvest the greatest kudos and number of votes for himself and, unlike the private business man, the politician reaps *his* reward before the consequences to the balance-sheet come to light. Benn was one of the rare individuals to be shown up. Reporting later, the Select Committee on Public Expenditure did not find much excuse for Benn because in December 1969 the IRC had certainly made it known to the government that millions would be required by Rolls Royce and that 'in our view Rolls Royce was not a viable entity'. Benn's response was to attack. He claimed that Heath's industrial policy was as bankrupt as Rolls Royce and that 'without the RB-211 engine there is no future for the British aeroengine industry, whether in public ownership or not'. He went on to claim that the credibility of the whole British aircraft industry had been destroyed by the Government's action and that future sales of Concorde and the Harrier jump jet were put in jeopardy. This drew cheers from his supporters but Chancellor of the Exchequer Anthony Barber's indictment of Benn's monumental mistakes were what remained in the memory and stole newspaper headlines

— except in the *Morning Star* which did its best to make the whole thing look like a Benn triumph.

Concorde was another of the 'advanced technology' projects which Benn had had an important part in fostering, but which from his point of view always contained the seeds of disaster. Not only did the costs keep on bounding ahead of estimates, but the plane was also being made in Bristol on Benn's doorstep. The danger in early 1970 was that American East Coast environmentalists would kill it off. Their case, put before the New York State Assembly in February, alleged that North Hampstead, a township on the edge of Kennedy Airport, would be subjected to excessively high noise levels from Concorde. More serious than the court case was the bill to limit aircraft noise being put forward by a member of the State legislature, Mr Andrew Stein. In a bid to stop the bill, which could become law within weeks, Benn went to New York, accompanied by another Bristol MP — the Conservative Robert Adley. Before leaving, Benn issued a statement in London warning the Americans against denying Britain and France the fruits of ten years of effort as well as the expenditure of £500 millions. Yet this was only one in a series of rearguard actions fought against Concorde, and even if this one was fought off, there were other shots in the environmentalists' locker. In fact the previous April a leading American scientist, Dr Harold Johnson of the University of California, reported to President Nixon that a world fleet of 500 supersonic transports could halve the ozone content of the atmosphere in less than a year. This would result in all the animals in the world being blinded if they lived out of doors in day light and the view of some of Dr Johnson's colleagues was that it could mean the death of all plant life as well. It was enough to make even a politician with constituents' jobs at stake think twice.

Of all the great white elephants forged in the white heat of the technological revolution promoted during Benn's time at Min Tech there was none to compare with the Shipbuilders of Upper Clyde. When *The Times* announced that the Tories

were giving the naval shipyard at Yarrow £4.5 million (out of
the Ministry of Defence budget) to help them to break away
from the UCS Group in which they had been unhappy
partners, Benn, ever on the attack, accused them of
'presiding over the total shambles of an industrial policy'. Mr
John Davies, the Secretary of Trade and Industry, coldly
replied that Benn had put £20 million into UCS 'without due
regard for the real viability of these concerns,' and that 'The
clear purpose of the Government is not to bail out concerns
which cannot see their way through to viability.' So it was
no surprise when in mid June he announced that, determined
not to throw good money after bad, he was going to put UCS
into liquidation. Estimates varied as to how many jobs were
at risk, from 2500 in the *Economist* to 27 000 by Benn. This
was the policy of refusal to help industrial lame ducks with a
vengeance! Yet it was the fourth time that UCS had come to
the Government cap in hand and if in the years since the
rescue operation had begin, productivity in the yards had
indeed risen, it had been dearly bought since costs had risen
at least as much. Benn of course denounced the decision in
hysterical terms and when a few days later 100 000 Scots took
the afternoon off to protest for the right to work, Benn was
up in Glasgow to lead about 2500 of them through the city
centre, arms linked — in best 'Red Flag' tradition — with the
joint shop stewards committee. He had already told them a
few days earlier, when they came to London to protest to the
Prime Minister, that they should return to work immediately
at their UCS Yards. 'They are your yards', he said and added
that their fight was only a part of the wider struggle against
unemployment which the Labour party had to continue 'until
we get this government out'. Whether or not Benn put the
idea of a work-in into their heads, this was the beginning of
an important new phase when the Government's
determination to stop subsidising lame ducks was to be
eroded and a new myth created about the workers running
the shipyards themselves.

Meanwhile MPs were off for their summer recess. Labour

had called a special conference for mid-July on the Common Market at Central Hall Westminster. Harold Wilson came along and gave a tortuous speech, though one message at least was spelt out clearly — that on the terms which the Tories had agreed, the EEC was an unacceptable ramp. The conference agreed with him, but Mr. Callaghan said that deferring a decision until the autumn when the regular annual party beano took place would still give them plenty of time to decide, and that was the way the conference decided to vote. It was all, as George Brown had described it in advance, an absurd waste of time and notable only for the sweltering heat in which it was conducted; the delegates took off their jackets, revealing Mr Tom Dorking in a blood red shirt and Tony Benn competing in one of buttercup yellow.

It was after this occasion that Benn became the new Chairman of the Labour party. It was an opportunity which he used throughout his year of office to further extremist policies. He began as he clearly meant to go on, with a message on the eve of the annual Tolpuddle Martyrs demonstration and rally at Dorchester, in which he likened the plight of the dockers who had just been sent to jail, to that of the six Dorset men who were transported to Australia in 1834 for attempting to form a trades union. He went into a long historical homily to the effect that all our freedoms in Britian had been due to the protesters against the possessors of privilege who always reacted by calling the protest 'anarchy'. 'The law which put these men in prison was an evil law, drawn up by a government which hates the trades unions and is being enforced by lawyers who have no experience of the problems of working people and their families.' However, the dockers concerned were hardly heroic and their imprisonment was for contempt of court in a case arising from a dispute involving the picketing and blacking of cold stores. Benn's attitude was calculated to confer respectability on those who defied the law in blatant pursuit of their sectional interest. It could also be seen as part of a philosophy according to which no law is valid unless it is sanctioned by consensus, but this position, which is arguable, easily becomes the questionable doctrine that the unions must give their consent to any law affecting them. In other words, they should have a veto over laws which touch their interests, occupying a sort of no-go area for the legislators and lawyers 'who have no experience of the problems of working people'. Once accepted, the principle of such a *liberum veto* for interest groups over laws affecting themselves should not only apply to unions but also to surtax payers or indeed any taxpayers, as well as property developers, speculators, sub contractors on the 'Lump' and owners of shares in hived-off subsidiaries of nationalised industries. Benn's application of this principle of government by consent would not however appear to extend to such cases.

At the end of July, there was a further development in the continuing saga of Upper Clyde when John Davies announced that two of the three UCS shipyards were to be sold off and 400 of the 8500 workers made redundant immediately. Benn immediately claimed that 6000 workers would lose their jobs and that this would be a major tragedy for the men involved and for Scotland'. Mr Davies replied, 'Your characteristic exaggeration seeks to duck your own manifest responsibility for the situation.' On the Upper Clyde itself there followed a workers' occupation of the yards and the shop stewards committee told the liquidator that they would dictate 'all future policy'. Benn was up in Glasgow to encourage them and made a bitter attack on Lord Robens, one of the four Government-appointed advisers who had recommended that the Upper Clyde consortium should be broken up, describing the advisers' report as 'this cheap slip of paper' and 'simply a hatchet job by these people for the Government — the most disreputable report ever published in Parliament'. John Davies, who had come late to Parliament from being Director General of the CBI and was not a noted orator, was stung into probably his best speech up to that moment when he addressed the emergency Commons debate on the 2 August. He called Benn 'the evil genius of shipbuilding — he sponsored and encouraged the whole ill-fated venture ... his present behaviour is an affront to all that has gone before'. Benn had indeed admitted at the opening of the debate that creating the group was a mistake, but it was an admission only in the totally unsatisfactory sense that 'it would have been better had the Government taken the whole industry into public ownership. We could then have re-equipped it, rationalised it and swept away many of the old ogres.' This hardly amounted to anything more than a reassertion that nationalisaton was the panacea. There was no mention of how this panacea would solve the real problem of overmanning — only that putting public money into the Group would be easier if it were publicly owned. This indeed was true, but no comfort to the taxpayers who had to foot the bill.

Still, if accounts and indeed accountability, were not Benn's strong suit, protest and demagogy were, and Scotland beckoned. Back up there for a protest march by 50 000 on 18 August, he made an inflammatory speech about Heath's attempted 'murder' of UCS and somebody with a sense of occasion lobbed a smoke bomb on to the platform though no one was hurt. This attack on Heath was indeed Benn's own smoke bomb to divert attention from the fact that the real guilt was his own. In shouting for more support from public funds, it was very convenient for Benn to forget that in 1969 he had been the one to say, 'we have never taken the view that at whatever price UCS or any other company in the shipbuilding industry would be kept alive'.

Benn returned to the stump at the Labour party conference in October, saying of the Upper Clyde work-in that 'the workers in UCS have done more to advance the cause of industrial democracy in ten weeks than all the Labour party's blueprints of the last ten years'. This was all in aid of the myth he was keen to foster that the workers had taken over the shipyards and the myth was helped by television coverage which showed the shop stewards meeting in the boardroom. However all the while the yards were actually being run by the liquidator, and the more than 6000 men who went on working in the yards were paid out of government funds or out of debts collected by the liquidator. Jimmy Reid, the Communist leader of the joint shop stewards committee, also proved a sympathetic television personality, and was constantly displayed to the viewing public while government spokesmen brought on to reply were disappointingly defensive. Perhaps this was because the Government's own resolution was crumbling. It was the Upper Clyde dispute and the Government's failure to stick to its guns which broke the credibility of its anti-inflationary policy. Heath's alleged toughness proved, when put to the test, to be very brittle. The demonstrations, plus the figures for Glasgow unemployment soon broke his resolve. The UCS story was not over yet, but its importance as a milestone, or rather a gravestone, of the Conservative government's silent revolution cannot be exaggerated. Only in the most narrowly party sense then could Benn consider the UCS episode a victory, but in the year of his chairmanship, even more than usual, one would expect him to be partisan. Certainly there was no lack of further excitement.

There were opportunities galore for addressing protest meetings, regarded as the very models of political activity by Benn, now well into his grass roots democrat phase — giving release to the spirit of the people, letting it well up from below to buoy him up, sustain him, inspire him. One example of this was the meeting in Trafalgar Square in support of the miners' strike in February 1972, where Benn delivered a fine tirade against Edward Heath and this time said something perceptive instead of merely sensational: 'Mr Heath's greatest weakness', he said, 'is that he simply does not understand people. If people get in his way he simply brushes them aside. He is a cold, hard man, leading a cabinet of cold, hard men.' This last bit went a bit too far. If they had been a bunch of cold hard men, they might have got somewhere, but in fact they were supersensitive to gusts of public opinion, all the more so because most of them were pragmatists

e: Workers' solidarity.
hadow Industry Minister
protesting UCS workers
wning Street. On his left,
Jeffer MP; on his right,
s Skinner MP.
al Press Photos)

* The burdens of office?
arty Chairman surveys the
Labour conference.
Association Photos)

Top: The inside story? The Industry Minister and Sir Don (now Lord) Ryder at the press conference on the Ryder Report on British Leyland *(Central Press Photos)*

Bottom: The outside story? At an anti-EEC press conference with (centre) Peter Shore MP and (right) Judith Hart MP. *(Daily Telegraph)*

concerned with holding office rather than fulfilling a task. Benn voiced the contempt of the crusader, however wrong-headed, for the time-server. Then triumphantly he concluded, 'if there is one message which has come from this meeting, it is that we should have a general election'. There was also the party's relationship with the unions to be borne in mind. In a fraternal address to the Trades Union Congress in September 1972, remembering the ill-fated attempt of Barbara Castle to impose legal responsibilities on the unions, he appealed for a new start and promised a total rejection of any interference with collective bargaining such as was being practised by the Tory government. 'We shall certainly reject a general freeze, overall statutory restraint, any system which penalises the lower paid, and the whole idea that wages are the sole, or even the principal, cause of inflation.' All very fine, until a Labour government was returned and imposed wage restraints not by statute but by administrative blackmail all in an attempt, so it said, to help the lower-paid worker.

Much of Benn's energy was taken up with the Common Market on which issue at least it would be unjust to label him an extremist. His formal position was indeed that he was in favour, though he had moved like a weathercock from one side to the other in the preceding years. He was more properly called a populist because his overriding aim was to have the matter of Britain's membership of the Community decided by referendum. At the outset it looked as if here was an issue on which he was not going to get his way because Harold Wilson was opposed to it but fate played into his hands. When President Pompidou decided to let the French people determine by referendum whether the British should join, it seemed on the face of it ridiculous that the same facility should not be extended to the British themselves. The argument was hard to refute and served him well when he was rebuked by the Dutch Socialist President of the European Commission, Dr. Mansholt in April for his nationalism in standing against the Community idea. For he was able to reply that it was not nationalism, but democracy which was his guiding light.

All this is however to ignore the usefulness of the Common Market controversy in isolating Benn's enemies on the Labour Right. There is no doubt that there were real advantages to be gained in opposing the policy of entering the Common Market on Tory terms, for all its humbug — exposed by Labour's George Thomson, who said that when Wilson applied in 1965, he would have been glad to accept the terms which Heath had obtained. The prime advantage, though, was that it put Roy Jenkins and the other Social Democrats in the party — who were virtually all ardent marketeers — on the spot as far as the internal party struggle was concerned. Jenkins had indeed begun the year of Benn's chairmanship with some measure of success by being re-elected very nearly outright as Labour's deputy leader. The pressure within the Labour party was however to oppose the policy to which the Tory Prime Minister, like Jenkins, was particularly attached. This struggle over whether or not to stay in the EEC had all sorts of complicated side effects and for instance, it was probably the factor which finally prevent Gwyn Morgan, a Common Market supporter and friend of Roy Jenkins, from becoming the Labour party's General Secretary in March 1972. The vote between Gwyn Morgan and Ron Hayward, who was preferred by the Left, was a tie, and Benn, as Chairman, used his casting vote in favour of Hayward. That was just a straw in the wind which was blowing Jenkins into isolation as the supporter of a main plank of Tory policy. Jenkins and his close supporters eventually voted in the Commons against the majority of the Labour party in favour of joining the Common Market (though in the first instance on 17 February against it) and his undertaking afterwards not to vote for the legislation consequential upon joining looked like a rather shabby compromise by one who was determined to cling, if not to office, then the prospect of office. Even this position was not tenable for long, and Jenkins soon felt obliged to resign from the Shadow Cabinet, followed by a number of sympathisers

— including Dick Taverne, George Thomson and Dr David Owen.

The case of Dick Taverne was particularly interesting because his support for the Common Market policy upset his Labour party executive at Lincoln so much that they decided not to adopt him at the next election. Taverne appealed to the National Executive, and when the case finally came before that body Benn made at least two speeches so hostile to Taverne that Denis Healey accused him of abusing his position as party Chairman. The decision went against Taverne and in October he decided to leave the Labour party to resign and fight his seat as a 'Democratic Labour Candidate' in the ensuing by-election which, despite bitter campaigning speeches against him by Benn, he won handsomely. Even if that was something of a setback for Benn, in the context of the struggle for the soul of the Labour party, it was a huge success for the Left and the beginning of the end of Labour's social democratic wing. Benn followed his victory on the policy of non-support for the Tory policy of joining the Community by pushing successfully for non-cooperation by Labour MPs by refusing to serve in the European Parliament, hoping to induce leading members of the Community to respond to Labour's determination and renegotiate seriously.

In the months following Labour's defeat Benn had rarely been out of the headlines and his standing in the party was high. But as we shall see in the next chapter, his inept handling of the 1972 party conference was somewhat to dent his image; in the event, this was a temporary set-back from which he recovered, and after his year as party Chairman ended he continued to give a lead to Labour's attack on a Tory government which was increasingly losing the courage of its waning convictions.

7

SMITING
THE TORIES
1972~4

Before examining Benn's activities in the year before the 1974 miners' strike, it is instructive to consider his chairmanship of the party conference of 1972 — the climax of his year as Chairman — which did not, as it turned out, say much for the practicality of his much publicised ideals of participatory democracy.

There seems little doubt that in the run-up to the conference his elevated position went to Benn's head. It was not the first time such a thing had happened: Harold Laski had the same vainglorious idea when he became Chairman under Attlee, though the latter alternately ignored his Chairman or slapped him down. Benn, perhaps merely intent on pushing his theories of popular democracy and participation — for there is a definite element of naivety in Benn's make-up — announced a week before the conference was due to begin that if delegates should vote against entry into the Common Market on principle, that decision must be accepted by a future Labour government. Roy Jenkins made the rather telling rejoinder that Benn had been rooting over the past year for a referendum despite the fact that the previous party conference had voted two to one against it, so he was himself defying a conference vote. This time, however, Benn seems to have realised that he had gone too far. Instead of beginning the party conference with a rabble-rousing appeal to the delegates to make sure that the leadership did as it was told once conference had pronounced, he made the deliberate disclaimer, 'conference never has and never will want to dictate to a Labour government . . . But,' he went on, 'they do expect Labour governments to take conference decisions seriously and not deliberately reverse or ignore them.' Just as well for Benn that he made his retreat in time, because if he had any idea of displacing Wilson as Labour's leader he was soon to learn the results of a public opinion poll which showed that the incumbent had the backing of seventy-nine per cent of Labour voters. Just to rub it in Ted Short, the party's deputy leader, when asked what he thought of Benn's chances, replied he did not think he was a front runner at all.

Whatever hopes Benn had of the conference as far as projecting his own image, in the event it was a bit of a flop. The trouble was that Benn got it into his head that he should not be a managing sort of a chairman, but a kind of passive medium through whom the people channelled their intentions, for he believed the best sort of leader in a democracy is so unnoticed as to be virtually invisible. Unhappily for this scheme Benn overdid it. When he said in his final speech from the platform, 'Democracy is a rather messy business' Joe Gormley, the mineworkers' leader, was heard to growl, 'It would help if you didn't make such bloody silly rulings.' A joke made among his colleagues at the conference was that Benn was very fond of reading the works of Mao Tse Tung. 'A ha', said some of them, 'but he should read another chairman's work — Citrine's *ABC of Chairmanship.'* Certainly, his weakness in the chair led to far too many specious points of order being raised.

Silly or not, the motions passed by the conference were just what the doctor ordered as far as Benn was concerned, for they showed a distinct shift to the Left. The conference, by 4 174 000 to 1 000 000 (this was of course the card vote in operation) pledged the party to a policy of 'retrospectively relieving' any councillors who were paralysed financially for having refused to implement the Housing Finance Act. This was exactly in accordance with Benn's doctrine that defiance of the law was acceptable, even praiseworthy, if based upon conscience, and it had the additional merit from a radical's point of view that the motion was passed against the recommendations of the National Executive. The Executive were also defeated on the proposal to extend nationalisation in the building industry. The leftward drift was further confirmed by the elections to Labour's National Executive in which Denis Healey, who had often annoyed the Left during his time as a Minister of Defence managed to hold on to seventh place only by a beggarly 3000 votes.

If the content of the conference was satisfactory to Benn, the impression it gave to the public was not. Even so he might have pulled it together and restored his own reputation had he made the right speech at the end. Yet that is just what, uncharacteristically, he did not do. For he took it as the opportunity to make a bizarre attack on Dick Taverne for resigning his seat at Lincoln and fighting a by-election as a 'Democratic Labour' candidate, describing him as 'neither democratic nor Labour'. Even more foolishly he went on to attack the press, which, he insisted, had invented Taverne's party, the master inventor apparently being William Rees-Mogg, the Editor of *The Times*. He further alleged that the television companies were preparing a massive campaign in support of this the candidate which Fleet Street had promoted at Lincoln. It was in the course of his attack on the press and television that he made remarks which were widely interpreted as evidence of a desire to inaugurate a workers' censorship. His actual words were: 'I sometimes wish that trade unionists who work in the mass media—those who are writers, broadcasters, secretaries, printers and lift operators at Thompson House—would remember that they too are members of our working class movement and have a responsibility to see that what is said about us is true'. There were rousing cheers at the end of this oration, but it was a serious error and not surprisingly he took a terrible beating in the newspapers: the *Sun*, for example, editorialised scornfully, 'Come off it Wedgie . . . Dreaming up impossible press conspiracies is the first fantasy of every disappointed politician. Tony should know there is no truth in it and no mileage to be got out of it.' He was also generally condemned for attacking Taverne, whose sincerity was considered beyond dispute. Still worse, Harold Wilson was obliged to issue a statement disowning Benn's plea for shop floor censorship and making it clear that the Labour party was 'toally opposed in all circumstances to the use of industrial action for the purpose of impeding the printing or discrimination of news, or the expression of views'. Even before this, Benn had had to issue a denial that he was urging printers to strike against newpapers hostile to the Labour movement, but the damage was already done and nobody was convinced, nor should they have been, because the meaning of his words was quite clear.

The displeasure of his shadow cabinet colleagues was shown soon afterwards when his suggestion that the parliamentary party should oppose the Royal Assent to the European Communities Bill was snubbed. He was unpopular with Labour backbenchers as well and in the ballot for the annual election of the shadow cabinet he only just hung on in eleventh place. Nor did things improve in the House, where in a debate on Concorde in December Benn was suddenly seized with the urge to confess that when he had been the responsible Minister he had conducted secret negotiations with the French to the effect that either Government after 1969 could, under certain conditions, stop work on Concorde. As the *Evening Standard* observed, it was indeed a strange admission to come from this apostle of open government that he had kept parliament and his own constituents (many of them employed on Concorde) in the dark about this vital public issue.

The setback was however brief and Benn had not lost his resilience. Moreover, as front bench spokesman on Trade and Industry, he had plenty with which to occupy himself. At the end of January 1973 he was in the news again, denouncing Heath and asking with apparent indignation, why, since Nixon had decided to end the war in Vietnam, Heath did not follow his example and end his own war against the TUC? Next month he had the satisfaction of welcoming a policy document agreed in the TUC Labour party Liaison Committee, which promised a fiscal attack on the rich and a straitjacket for the economy in the form of statutory price control. Benn suffered another unexpected rebuff in March when Taverne won a sensational victory in the by-election at Lincoln. For Benn had gone on record at the previous party conference with his belief that not only would Taverne be crushed, but that Labour's victory would open the way to a general election in which they would sweep back to power.

Yet the tide of affairs *was* swinging Labour's way, and the most convincing argument was that the Heath government was also moving leftwards, (that is towards economic controls and interventionism) on which Benn seized very effectively in a long article in *The Sunday Times* in March, entitled 'Heath's Spadework for Socialism'. He was able to point gleefully to Peter Walker's plan for reorganising nuclear power, and Christopher Chataway's provision of millions of pounds of public money for a motor cycle merger, the £45 million given to the successor of UCS, the passing of the Industry Act, and, in some ways most important of all, powers taken to control prices and profit margins. Benn was eager that once the opportunity arose, Labour should use the instruments which Heath had created, and take the collectivist process further, with crucial importance being attached to nationalising the aircraft industry. This, he advocated, in a form which would include a large dose of industrial democracy, in a speech in April to a receptive

audience of shop stewards, said to represent 150 000 aircraft
workers. He once more threatened nationalisation without
compensation to those who bought shares in Rolls Royce.
This statement however suffered from factual inaccuracy for
Rolls Royce could not be renationalised since it had never
been taken into public ownership. The speech was not
without effect, for it scared the public off buying shares in
Rolls Royce, less than a fifth of the issue being taken up.
Here however he had gone ahead of his party, and though the
shadow cabinet would not agree on a statement, Wilson
issued one under his own name denying that Labour would
seize the shares of Rolls Royce without compensation. It
therefore almost like poetic justice when in early August there
came the inspectors' report on the bankruptcy of Rolls
Royce; this they attributed directly to the drain on the
company's resources caused by the RB-211 engine, which
Benn at the time had been so self-congratulatory about
supporting. It was a combination of the rashness of Sir
Denning Pearson and Benn's equally romantic enthusiasm
for the products of advanced technology which led to
disaster.

Some months earlier, the shadow Ministers had been
attending May Day celebrations, particularly lively on this
occasion because they coincided with a national strike against
the Government's pay and prices policy, for which 1 600 000
workers turned out. Benn, who was speaking at the
Birmingham rally, said that the strike was 'an educational
function for the benefit of the Government,' but the
Government persisted in going on as if impervious to the
lessons of this particular teach-in.

By June, the National Executive was ready to present its
plan for nationalising twenty-five of Britain's largest
companies. One major objection was that it would cost
£12 000 million, and was likely to lose Labour the next
general election. It was the second point which counted as far
as Wilson was concerned; not any issue of principle about
maintaining the mixed economy or avoiding over-

concentration of power, but purely the question of how it would affect the voters in the polling booth. In any case, Wilson put his foot down. Later other members of the shadow cabinet joined in denouncing the scheme (including Foot!), all anxious not to lose the election.

It was around this time that Benn, especially when talking to city businessmen, first used the phrase 'a fundamental and irreversible shift of power and wealth in favour of working people and their families'. Labour's programme was supposed to be the result of a large scale democratic exercise involving 1 000 people in constituencies, but it was all very vague as to who they were, and who was to supervise their work. In any case, the 1 000 participation figure was rather small. The Conservative Political Centre was at that time without a great deal of fuss doing such an exercise eight times a year and the number participating was of the order of 10 000. The Benn exercise was not in any case very democratic and the recommendations tended to reflect the left-wing views of the National Executive and the Labour party Research Department.

A public opinion poll at this juncture showed that in the popularity stakes Heath was trailing Powell. In the Labour Party, Wilson was still on top, followed by Callaghan, Jenkins and Castle, but Benn was just in the list, standing at number five.

The conference season was once again looming up and Benn, ever ready for a good publicity cry, found one in early September in the export of a computer to the South African authorities who used it to supervise their pass laws. He expressed shock at the discovery that this sale had been made in 1968 when he was responsible and said that when Labour returned to power there would be an embargo. This was a new and potentially fruitful field for Benn since capitalism is notoriously unconcerned with morality (though its immorality cuts both ways: an investigation into how many British firms export barbed wire to East Germany might prove interesting.

Harold Wilson was also planning for the party conference and in a crafty move tried to replace the pre-conference meeting of the National Executive with a joint meeting of that body with the shadow cabinet, the idea being to give a majority against the National Executive's proposal to nationalise twenty five leading companies — for which of course Benn was the leading campaigner. In the event, Wilson did not obtain his joint meeting but the pressure for it was probably the reason why the Executive finally agreed to oppose a resolution putting forward its own policy. Even so, Benn was busy preparing his own industry bill which would give power to a future Labour government to take over companies, replace directors, and prevent multinational concerns from switching their production to factories abroad to the detriment of British workers. At a Tribune eve-of-conference meeting, Ian Mikardo, one of the Benn faction, said that the party's new undertaking should not be limited to the takeover of the top twenty-five companies, or even the top 250, but should commit the next Labour government to 'a continuous process of nationalisation' which would over a period of two or three parliaments bring four-fifths of the economy under state control. So the twenty-five companies proposal was evidently not what it appeared at first to be. It was not only a new concept of a mixed economy with a more predominant public sector but also the thick end of the wedge — not so much a party programme, more the beginning of a Marxist way of life.

Of course, the conference had no diffulty in passing the nationalisation list, and when one came to look at it carefully, it was obvious that there would have been no point in the National Executive making a fuss about the twenty-five firms for there was no lack of scope for the nationalisers' itch. The menu included the docks, shipbuilding, North Sea and celtic oil and gas, some pharmaceuticals, some machine tools, building land, mineral resources, road haulage, aircraft production, parts of the construction industry and an open-ended commitment through a National Enterprise Board and

Benn's pet Industry Act to take over further key if unspecified private firms. In Benn's speech in the reply to the debate which preceeded the vote, one looked in vain for any economic justification, any suggestion that the firms taken over would, once in public ownership, become more efficient. The whole argument was emotive and concerned with Benn's theory of democracy. Either we control the big companies or they will control us was the theme, and there was one ominous pronouncement in particular which went down well with the delegates. This was, 'the crisis that we inherit when we come to power will be the occasion for fundamental change and not the excuse for postponing it'. Lenin himself could not have phrased it better. Without vision the people no doubt die, but with Benn there was precious little else, apart that is from sneers at Slater Walker and snarls at Fleet Street. Still, it was good from an oratorical point of view and he sat down to prolonged applause. One senior Labour MP, however, was not impressed after watching Benn's exhibition of boy scout fervour and said, 'If we do go down again at the next election, the guilt is going to be shared between the Powellites and the Baden Powellites'.

There were more votes to come to gladden the hearts of the Left — nuclear bases to be abandoned, public schools squeezed, Europe repudiated, the Housing Finance Act and the Industrial Relations Act eradicated. Above all there was Healey, often dubbed right-wing by commentators — perhaps because he had once been enthusiastic about defending the country — but there he was making a speech promising, amidst tumultuous cheers from the Left, levels of taxation which would provoke 'howls of anguish from the rich': a fearsome prospect to be sure when the rich in question appeared to be those with incomes in excess of £3000 a year!

Benn may have been flattered too to find that he had at this point in his career achieved wider recognition because he was included in an article in *Fortune,* the prestigious American business magazine, as one of the dramatis personae in an article entitled, 'The ominous forces of world socialism'. Fellow ominous forces were France's Mitterand, Australia's Whitlam and the head of West Germany's Young Socialists, Wolfgang Roth. *Fortune* described Benn as 'the charismatic star of the radical faction' and 'and aggressive activist', but suggested that some of the more dedicated radicals thought him an opportunist. Benn could at least take comfort from the fact that the NEC voted to continue the boycott of the European Parliament at Strasbourg, even if it did not accept his more radical proposal that a Labour government should freeze all payments to the Community during renegotiation. It was gratifying too that the previous year's shambles seemed to have been forgotten by the Labour conference and in the vote for the membership of the National Executive Benn came third.

All in all, it was a fine conference for Benn and company, but their satisfaction was not shared by the press or by the country at large. Evidence of this appeared in some by-elections shortly after the conference in which Labour performed badly, losing Govan in Scotland to a Scottish Nationalist candidate, showing up poorly at Berwick and Edinburgh North and, if it was no surprise, coming third at Hove, where the party experienced the extra humiliation of the Labour candidate actually losing his deposit. These misfortunes led to a good deal of strife in the Labour ranks, even among the officers. Reginald Prentice, one of the increasingly beleaguered social democrats, publicly denounced the 'half-baked Marxists and others hell-bent on nationalising everything'. Did this signify that social democrats in the party were finally going to fight, that they had at last taken alarm at Benn's frequent reiteration of his plan to achieve shifts of economic and social power which were 'irreversible', that they now realised how ominous the use of that word was and how much a denial of the parliamentary process by one who professed such attachment to it?

Alas no, but fortunately for Labour the Tories were having

similar troubles. Enoch Powell, maverick genius of the Tory right, commenting on a speech by Premier Edward Heath on the miners and the pay code remarked 'one cannot but entertain fears for the mental and emotional stability of a head of government to whom such language can appear rational'. As a matter of fact, the greatest threat to the mental and emotional stability of Mr Heath was Powell himself, whom the Tory leader regarded with a mixture of loathing and bewildered apprehension. But the point of contention was one on which, interestingly enough, Powell and Benn were at this time agreed and were forcefully making — that the pay and prices code did not have the force of law. It was only a chance conjunction: in their general conceptions of how the economy should be run they were like chalk and cheese. Powell was the arch apostle of the free market gospel, while Benn was the guru of interventionlism, and moreover interventionlism inspired overwhelmingly by political —that is ballot-box — considerations.

Benn's hyper-sensitivity to the claims of organisational interests with votes in tow was shown in his undertaking a couple of weeks later to Barry Jones, MP for East Flint, that the next Labour government would have a rethink about the closure of Shotton steel works by the British Steel Corporation. Benn's populism, his readiness to support any act of defiance by the workers against the management (defence of whom he was apt to describe scornfully as 'managerialism') and his self-identification with the cause of people clinging to jobs which could only be maintained by subsidy, had already given rise to a series of disastrous adventures with public money. But here he was again, like an unredeemed alcoholic, confident that all would be well after the next swig at the bottle.

Just before Christmas, 1973, Benn was away on another tack with a proposal from a party study group under his Chairmanship for the next Labour government to set up a commission on press reform. The main proposals were for: financial support of minority publications *(Gay News, Red*

Dwarf, Morning Star?); subsidies to launch, establish and
allow access to new entrants into the newspaper market; the
removal of the 'distortion' of advertising finance. To these
ends he proposed an Advertising Revenue Board, which was
to seize all the advertising receipts for press publications
direct from the advertiser or from his agent, charged by the
Board at full market rates (whatever 'market rates' might
mean in these circumstances). The publishers would then
receive a commission for the advertising fixed mainly in
relation to audited circulation figures. 'The advertiser would
be free to choose whatever media he wished, the newspaper
would be free to take as much advertising as it liked and the
space broker would be free to sell space. But the payments
would be made through the Board which would also have the
responsibility for fixing the rates, for research and
promotion, and would be staffed by people now working
within media organisations.' The idea of loading the press
with this extra layer of bureaucracy was apparently to weaken
the link between the wealth, social composition and influence
of readership and advertising revenues, and to render the
value of readers to a publication more equal (or more baldly,
to stop newspapers benefitting from providing the public
with what it wants to read). The Board would use its 'surplus'
to provide a development fund to enable new publications to
enter the market and would also operate a sliding scale for
newsprint prices so as to offset the normal effect of falling
unit costs as volume grows, the intention being to neutralise
the privilege of size. In effect the scheme would mulct the
professional and executive classes in order to subsidise the
kinds of publications (such as Trotskyist broadsheets) for
which most of them have no use.

Turning to broadcasting, the report promised an Executive
National Broadcasting Commission. This would collect
television revenue and allocate funds granted by Parliament
throughout the broadcasting industry. There would be two
television corporations, one to run a national, the other a
regional, channel along with one or two radio corporations.

Finance for broadcasting would come from television advertising revenue and, if necessary, from the Treasury. The license fee would be phased out, starting with its abolition for pensioners.

So there it was, Benn's scheme for the media, combining the economies of the madhouse with the politics of Big Brother. Plainly they did not call him 'Commissar' Benn for nothing and one could imagine him putting the scheme into operation, being frightfully reasonable about it all, perhaps getting a little tetchy at his great vision being misunderstood, but for the most part orating volubly and happily about improved communications with people in a socialist community while ruin spread all around.

The Benn frenzy was anyway now entering the manic stage as a general election loomed. Heath had got himself in deep water with his Keynesian dash for growth, and an inflationary nemesis was overtaking him, complicated further by the Arabs' decision to raise the price of their oil. The prices and incomes policy wished upon Heath (as on every other government from 1960 onwards) by an importunate and blinkered Whitehall, had finally thrust him into confrontation with the miners who were in a strong position to get what they wanted. One of the ways out, or so it seemed to many in the Conservative party at the time, was to go to the electorate with the cry 'Who rules? — the elected government or the unions?'. In such circumstances, with public excitement rising to fever pitch, the activist politician has his chance of making history or making a fool of himself. At Transport House they already realised that in the 1970 election Benn's hyperenergy misdirected to the point of genius against Enoch Powell very likely made all the difference between their failure and success. In the February 1974 election campaign things worked differently. As it turned out, Enoch was not the enemy but an ally — he told the electors to vote Labour and on the very grounds Benn would have most approved — the threat which the Common Market presented to the British people's freedom to determine their own destiny. Benn's instinct was to oppose the Tories on all points almost regardless of where this landed his party. Thus he was a moving spirit in the National Executive's decision in December to take a further step committing a future Labour government to remove retrospectively any penalties, financial or otherwise from councillors like those at Clay Cross, who defied the Housing Finance Act and to reimburse any fines imposed under the Act. As Labour's Research Department had discovered, some legal snags existed about repaying the fines since the conference's recommendation to the same effect, so the NEC resolution talked about a fighting fund to meet the Clay Cross Councillors' legal expenses.

The same tendency to take almost promiscuously the side of those who were *prima facie* lawbreakers emerged in his support for a dossier produced by Bristol trades council which alleged police harassment of left-wing groups and the misuse by the police of their powers. The National Council for Civil Liberties — a body with a record remarkable mainly for selectivity in the freedoms it supports, although its general tendency when in doubt is to side against the police — had been the originator of the complaints. It was a good subject on which to make a fuss and offered Benn opportunities to embroider his favourite theme about the need for less secrecy in government. The three men making accusations against the police were an International Socialist and two Maoists. Could it be that it was less a matter of harassment of left wingers and (especially when, say, one is looking for explosives) more a matter of one left-wing suspect often leading to another?

Meantime, Heath's confrontation with the miners had become serious and by December a three day week was brought in to avoid a breakdown of services due to lack of fuel. Benn questioned the decision and challenged the Government to produce figures of distributed stocks and deliveries of coal, but of course these were just what it did not want to reveal because that would have enabled the miners to assess their strength. With his usual flair for publicity Benn, allegedly because of the Government's refusal to answer his questions, announced that the Labour party was setting up its own information bureau. This was all good old party political knockabout stuff, but the same could not be said of Benn's next pronouncement in the New Year when he made the extraordinary assertion that the three day week was the Government's means of imposing a 'sharp and massive deflation'. This did not suggest a very sound grasp on Benn's part of the elementary laws of supply and demand for, on normal expectations, if a three day week led to a reduction of pay in many (but certainly not all) cases it could be expected to produce an even bigger fall in production, so the net effect would be not *de*flationary but *re*flationary. As it turned out (though Benn was not to know this) the three day week was actually less inflationary than might reasonably have been expected because in the emergency there was a general abandonment of restrictive practices (the main reason for Britain's poor industrial performance) and industrial production during the three day week, despite all the difficulties, was little changed from that of the full week — a wonderful pointer to what an economic miracle there might be if labour restrictions were permanently dropped. But Benn was going off like a firecracker by this time. There had to be a freeze, he asserted, on all mortgage payments, rents and hire purchase debts for the duration of the three day week, a recommendation which, if followed, would further limit the economy's adaptability just when that quality was most needed. In fact, Benn's fanatic views did not on this occasion attract a very good press even among those newspapers which usually supported him. The *Sunday Mirror* was particularly scornful:

'Does he smile wickedly to himself in the shaving mirror as he contemplates the ludicrous plot he has attributed to Mr Heath?

'Or does he believe the paranoid piffle he spouts

as Labour's spokesman?

'The *Sunday Mirror* fears he does. But that's no reason why anyone else should share his nightmares.'

Dick Taverne also bitterly attacked Benn: 'His problem is that he wants to be leader of the Labour party so badly that the truth is to be no obstacle'. Up to a point this was paying off an old score. Taverne had been helpful to Benn in the past, notably at the time when the latter was trying to divest himself of his title. Taverne had appeared before the Commons committee on privileges in the Benn interest and given a most erudite statement on medieval peerage law for which the Chairman, R.A. Butler, warmly thanked him. Benn's virulent personal attack on Taverne at the 1972 party conference must have hurt. Taverne not only hit back in words; he also put up a candidate in Benn's constituency which, that apart, was not looking at all secure. No wonder that when they by chance met in the corridors at Westminster they passed each other in silence.

The general line of Wilson and Benn throughout the strike was that the Government should give in to the miners' demands. As the *Yorkshire Post* happily put it 'In place of strife, capitulation'. Few paused to note that the most severe problem of inordinate wage demands was coming in the public sector, the massive extension of which Benn saw as the answer to the nation's problems.

If Heath had been wise and listened to the advice of the Conservative party professionals, he would have gone to the polls on the 7 February and probably won. Instead he went on the 28, when the three day week had started to bite, and duly lost. Benn, unlike Wilson, seems to have seen this coming. With prophetic insight on the first day of the campaign he said to a meeting in Halifax, 'Small businessmen fearing bankruptcy will not vote for Heath'. He then spoilt the effect of this perceptive comment by adding another dotty suggestion of a Tory plot by which through the three day week wealth and income were being redistributed to the better off, though this seems to have had for its only basis a statistically unsound article by Michael Meacher.

Benn was distinctly worried this time about holding his majority of 5600 in Bristol and told one reporter on the train that his chances were fifty-fifty. One idea he hit on was to have Roy Jenkins send him a message of support so as to reassure right-wing Labour people and others who suspected his radical views. Jenkins, whose pitch Benn had done so much to queer, coolly responded with a telegram saying 'My call to the electors of Bristol is to give their support to you as to the other official Labour candidates'. Benn, thankful even for this, replied with an effusive telegram of thanks, itself thirteen words longer than Jenkins' original message. Benn had in fact, been asking for support from all sorts of people, ranging from Trevor Huddlestone, Bishop of Stepney, to Clive Dunn, the actor in the *Dad's Army* television series. This was just an example of how he was throwing everything into the fight at Bristol, including even the park bench on which he had proposed to his wife Caroline in 1948 — a picture of which appeared in his election leaflet. Nor was it all in vain. Helped no doubt by the presence of a Liberal candidate, Benn actually increased his majority over the Conservatives by more than 2000 votes. So he was back after all and with every expectation of cabinet office.

8

INDUSTRY'S
MR. BIG

1974

The sudden downfall of Heath's government in 1974 seemed to confirm Benn's diagnosis that the British people would not be deterred by Labour's radical programme. In one respect he was profoundly right: the elector in these islands is most of the time a pragmatic soul who takes party manifestos with a large pinch of salt, voting when the time comes according to ancient, often inherited loyalty and only changing because annoyed with the Government for doing badly or, less often, because pleased by its doing well. Even then, his usual protest generally takes the form of not voting at all. That at least had been the rule until the 1974 election, when the floating voters, as they are misleadingly called (since it is not the same group of electors which changes each time) plumped in large numbers for the fringe parties — the Liberals winning 19.3 per cent of the votes cast and assorted celtic nationalists 5.4 per cent. Given the further fact that the Conservatives actually took more votes than Labour, no-one could seriously maintain that this was a case of the British electorate going overboard on Labour's scheme for a fundamental and irreversible shift of power in favour of the working class. It could more plausibly be interpreted as a declaration of no confidence in the major parties which both offered state collectivism.

In any event, whatever the larger logic of the election, Benn was back and appointed Secretary of State for Industry. His Ministry was carved out of the unwieldy Trade and Industry conglomerate over which Peter Walker had presided, (which was now split into Industry, Trade, Energy, and Prices and Consumer Protection) and, Benn now occupied the office suite in Victoria Street from which Walker had withdrawn. The Benn that emerged in the House of Commons after this preliminary takeover was not immediately recognisable as the zealot members had known and increasingly dreaded with the passage of time. It was a new conciliatory, self-deprecating, almost apologetic Benn. As the *Guardian* put it at the time, 'His speech in the House yesterday was placatory to the point of humility. When he said with some world-weariness, that "almost everything has been tried at least once" and was rewarded with a Conservative shout of "including you" Mr Benn managed a graceful smile.' It was hard to believe that the softly-softly style which had been imposed on him by Mr Wilson at the election had in the three-week campaign become consolidated into habit. More likely, the razor-thin majority of the Government, combined with his own apparently genuine preference for the persuasive had induced Benn to believe that this was not the time to wave the big long stick. There was also the certainty that the reports reaching him from industry must have been disturbing. Industry was suffering from a hangover after the three day week, inflation was rampant, and political uncertainty was extreme. It was obvious to the whole Labour cabinet that this was no time wantonly to undermine business confidence any further. Benn had every incentive, as well as no doubt every sort of advice from his colleagues, not to upset the apple-cart before the next election, which must come sooner rather than later. So the order of the day was be friendly to business. He even managed to be civil, to the extent of talking of the need for cooperation, to the CBI, though in a thoroughly partisan manner, by saying that there must never be another confrontation as occurred with the Industrial Relations Act.

The heady days of popular confidence in the prospects for government-sponsored technology, white-hot, luke-warm, or whatever, were gone. Indeed, the bones of the skeletons in the advanced technology cupboard where Benn had left them were rattling ominously. None more than Concorde, a source of increasing embarrassment to him, with its extra constituency dimension. Yet, as one of the principals in the promotion of the project he could hardly afford to ignore the disturbing evidence of mounting cost to the taxpayer, especially in view of the position he had recently assumed of champion of open government. He therefore determined on the bold course of publicising his agonising reappraisal of the project, including the possibility of even writing it off. On the figures he had given the House in March there was indeed a strong case for doing so. Already £500 million had been spent on design and development and further development would cost, at 1974 prices, an extra £200 million at least. Yet the operating costs too were enough to scare the airlines, none of which was likely to buy it unless arms were twisted. It was not as if Benn was worried about offending the French; being rude to a Common Market partner would be a bonus. On the other hand, for £80 million the redundancy costs could all be cleared away. It was beginning to look like a better and better option. So Benn managed to look very concerned, very wise and very occupied on weighing up the costs and benefits by the most refined and advanced methods of social accounting — and decided in the end to do nothing. While this was going on he also ordered the nationalised Steel Corporation to review urgently its planned steel closures — which was double-talk for *halting* steel closures — while he thought of something, or until an election took place. After all, the bill for the taxpayer would not come in until later. Not that Benn consciously thought in such terms; almost certainly he did not, but zeal can blind perception or at least allow those who possess or are possessed by it to see only what they wish to see.

Benn the crusader for, and ideologist of, socialism was not to be silenced for long. Fortified in April by an economic adviser from the Fabian Society, Mrs Frances Morell, and by Mr Francis Cripps from that seminary of dirigisme, the Department of Applied Economics in Cambridge (apparently advisers' salaries are not disclosed — open government is all right for some!), he was soon laying down the law again, this time on business. Perhaps they helped him produce the statistics for his speech on the 5 May, when he asserted that industry had received over £3 billion in subsidies in the previous four years which was equal to a half of what it had paid in taxes. This, he said, flying off at another tangent, amounted to half of what was paid to shareholders, so 'government was financing just under half the payment of dividends to shareholders', though he failed to mention that these in turn were taxed at a discriminatory rate. Moreover, the £3 billion, large as it was, was paid out for 'social engineering' purposes, that is to say, grants were given to companies only on certain conditions, such as their being prepared to invest in a factory in the celtic fringe. In other words the companies were as entitled to their grants as the unemployed worker to his dole. It was good propaganda though when directed at those who knew no better and a useful launching pad for the other Labour plans for setting up a National Enterprise Board and for putting individual firms into straitjackets called 'planning agreements'. As Benn well understood, these controls were not to be judged just for their value in promoting industrial investment but as a means of wrecking Tory finances since these planning agreements would be used to question and even stop donations to political parties. Since a large part of the Tory party's funds was still coming from companies, this opened up the exciting possibility of putting the enemy's political machine on short commons. It might also have dawned on some of the Conservatives who had been so eager to promote growth under the Heath government through various state subventions to private industry, that this only in the end threw themselves into the arms of Benn and Co. as Benn's criticism of industry having half what it paid in taxes back in grants did have a certain point when those firms were shouting about threats to free enterprise while in partnership with Heath they were conniving at the destruction of free enterprise. The real answer in terms of the competitive ethic was to do away with the grants altogether and halve the taxes at the same time. It is a measure of the degree to which their whole outlook has been socialised that many professed Conservatives would even now think such a suggestion preposterous.

The ideologist in Benn (which, by this time, was never far removed from that other element in his make-up, that is, Benn the unions' friend) broke surface also in denunciation of defence deals with Chile and South Africa. In mid May, he wanted to order a total ban on the modernisation of naval ships for the Chilean military Junta, being carried out on the Clyde and in this was supported by Hugh Scanlon, leader of the Amalgamated Union of Engineers who ordered his members to stop all work on Chilean contracts. The more immediate issue was whether the Cabinet should allow the refitting of thirty-nine Hawker Hunter fighter aircraft which had been sold to Chile years before. Foreign Secretary Jim Callaghan felt, on the whole, that the contract should go ahead because he feared that any interference would damage the large trade with other South American countries and apart from anything else the Chileans might hit back by cutting off supplies of copper. Mr. Wilson, still Prime Minister at this time, actually wrote to Ministers to remind them that they should assume their part of collective cabinet responsibility for the joint decision to go through with the contracts. A parallel row developed three days later over arms for South Africa, which came to a head when the British Aerospace Companies applied to Benn for permission to compete for arms contracts due to be put out for tender by the South African government in the next few weeks. Despite the value of the contract — about £500 million — he rejected the application out of hand.

Benn was not universally popular in the country at this juncture; one pointer to the negative esteem in which he was held in at least one part of Fleet Street was the suggestion in the *Daily Express* that he should be made Secretary of State for Northern Ireland in place of the plodding Merlyn Rees. The Daily Express argued, solicitously, that Benn was a 'strong minister with unbounded energy and enthusiasm who can meet the challenge of the stricken province'.

It was now that Benn re-emerged in his chosen role as the saviour of industrial lame ducks. He denounced the closure of Beaverbrook Newspapers in Glasgow and the making of 800 workers there redundant as 'barbaric'. He gave moral support and hinted at financial support as well for the mooted launching of a workers' co-operative to relaunch the paper as the *Scottish Daily News*. In June his Department announced its first intervention in industry when it took a fifty per cent stake in Kearney and Tricker Marwin — a high technology machine tool group, part of a £3½ million rescue operation. The object was to prevent the parent company, Vickers, dealing with the problem of a cash shortage (which at this time was starting to affect a great deal of British industry) by the more drastic solution of redundancy for some of the company's work-force of 1200 — most of them in Brighton. The latter was a small enough transaction, carried out interestingly enough under the powers given by the Heath government's Industry Act. Much more alarming were Benn's proposals put forward characteristically in a speech to the Nottinghamshire Miners Gala. He said that private industry stood indicted because of its failure to invest and that the Government was still considering the 'practical advantage' of extending the public sector. 'It is', he said, 'a tried and trusted system.' He then spelt it out that the advantages of the public sector were that it continued to invest and re-equip. It was a typical Bennite propaganda ploy, sticking to one main point — clear, simple and wrong. Private industry invests mainly out of profits when there are the prospects of profit. The nationalised industries can indeed invest, even though, as is very frequently the case, they are making losses, because they can tap the pockets of the taxpayer or, put another way, they can through the tax system get their hands on the money being made by the profitable firms in the private sector.

Further nationalisation Benn expected, but on top of that, Labour had plans for what private industry remained which they published in a Green Paper: *The Community and the Company,* in June 1974. It took its cue from the ideas of an earlier committee of left wingers, including Benn, which recommended forcing private industry to adopt an over-simplification of the West German two-board system with fifty per cent of the seats on the supervisory board being held not by workers but union representatives. This would amount to a complete takeover of companies by the union chiefs. It was not nationalisation in the ordinary sense, just a straightforward annexation and an outright gift to the union bosses of half the best non-executive industrial jobs in the country. It was also a sentence of death for the mixed economy. What industrial commissar could wish for more?

In the light of all this it meant very little for Benn to profess in the same month when opening a Bristol small firms information centre that he was 'all for free enterprise and small firms', since it was true only in the sense that it was the big firms and particularly the 100 biggest on which he wanted to put the thumbscrews. Perhaps too it was to mollify those cabinet colleagues who thought he was going to extremes in his proposals. Shirley Williams, one of the leading social democrats in the Cabinet, told the press after the August Cabinet meeting to finalise the White Paper on nationalisation that she understood public fears of 'a major extension of unrestricted state power', and went on, 'I would myself not wish to see that, any more than I would wish to see any further concentration of private power in our society.' So

Shirley made her protest but the Benn proposals were substantially unchanged. Much was made in the press of the 'dilution of Labour's plans for nationalisation', that is its agreeing to drop the naming of the companies in which the NEB might take an immediate interest or to specify the industrial sectors in which it would operate. Yet that did not amount to much, as the NEB would still have nationalisation *à la carte*. Meanwhile the commitments to nationalise shipbuilding, marine engineering, ports and aircraft industries, and to planning agreements for the largest companies survived unscathed. When it came to the crunch Shirley Williams, Roy Jenkins, Anthony Crosland and Bill Rogers had no idea of drawing the line and saying 'so far and no further'. Benn knew he had won and did not mind making a few agreeable noises so that the party could present a united front, especially with an election due. It was not before time therefore that Aims of Industry, a business-sponsored organisation, launched a £100 000 campaign against nationalisation or, as it was more and more coming to be called, 'Bennery'. Among other things, Aims was urging companies to oppose Benn's plans to lecture management and workers on the Government's strategy by refusing to make facilities available. 'You don't invite the executioner to tea,' an Aims spokesman crisply observed.

Benn was probably, if anything, encouraged at having more attention drawn to his plans and was found at the end of July fervently advocating the nationalisation of the shipbuilding industry. At this stage, shipbuilding, though not exactly one of the showpieces of British industry, was at least favoured by long order books which could well grow shorter at the prospect of the upheaval necessarily involved in a state takeover. The best that could be said for the scheme was that at market value the state would certainly be acquiring them cheaply, as Chancellor Healey, by depriving British business of much of its cash flow by his sharp increase in company taxes, had steeply raised the bankruptcy rate and brought about a severe stock market slump, bringing prices to their lowest since 1959. He was reining in the money supply all right, but in such a manner as to bring about general ruin in the business world, and it was already clear that he would soon have to bring in an autumn mini-budget in order to undo the damage wreaked in the spring. There was some fleeting, if grim, amusement however to be derived from the fact that the publication of Benn's proposals in August for more nationalisation was threatened by a shortage of supplies of the White Paper — because there was a strike at HM Stationery Office printers!

An election was clearly imminent in the autumn because the Government needed a larger working majority, while the opinion polls, which Harold Wilson pored over like a professional punter studying form, indicated that Labour had a commanding lead. A decisive factor in their favour was a negative one — the public dislike of Ted Heath. According to a poll in June carried out by Opinion Research Centre, nearly half the electors thought that it would be a good thing if Heath were replaced as leader of his party. Obviously in this electoral prelude the usual holiday from politics, which even the most dedicated MPs normally manage to enjoy during the summer recess, was not going to be available, and, as it turned out for Benn in particular, it proved to be a long hot summer in which he came nearer to being roasted than if merely exposed to scorching sun and sand.

The trouble arose over a leading British travel company called Court Line. In mid-August 1974, just after Benn's announcement of his ambitious programme of nationalisation, Court Line crashed, leaving 49 000 holiday makers stranded abroad. It was then recalled that Benn (who was at this juncture busily disclaiming responsibility) had earlier made a statement which had reassured 150 000 people who were in the course of booking holidays, and persuaded many to go ahead with them. He had said that the bookings were stabilised on the basis of his £24 million scheme to nationalise Court Line's sixteen shipbuilding companies. To make matters worse, only hours before the collapse, Benn had held up the example of the Government's support of Court Line as evidence of its ability to handle special situations of company difficulty. It was not a brilliant advertisement of how to conduct the open government for which Benn professed such attachment when Labour MP Ivor Clemitson complained that people had been kept in the dark and that for a number of weeks there had been a lack of information, 'a wall of silence'. Again it appeared that Benn had been in too much of a hurry. It now appeared that Mr Nicholson, the Rolls Royce receiver and an accountant from Peat Marwick and Mitchell under the Official Receiver, had been called in to investigate Court Line's financial position on 1 July, four days after Benn had made his speech which holiday tour bookers had taken to be a guarantee that all was well. It looked as if 100 000 people who had booked and were waiting to go on holiday with the group were going to lose both their holiday and their money. It was an opportunity of which Michael Heseltine, Tory Industry spokesman, took full advantage and issued a hard-hitting statement to the press pointing to the incongruity of Benn's far-reaching nationalisation plans and his amateur misjudgement in his dealings with Court Line. A further embarrassment arose when the pilots of the line said that Mr Clinton Davis, a junior trade minister had assured them early in July that passengers booked to travel would be safeguarded by government support in the form of a £4 million loan.

While all this was going on, Benn had the gall to make a speech at Coventry stating that his decision to give £5 million aid to the workers' co-operative at the Meriden motor cycle plant was 'a great turning point in British industry'. Or perhaps it was a turning point — but patently not for the better. That the Court Line affair would not be allowed to rest was quickly shown by the action of Mr William David Swain from Mobberley, Cheshire, who took out a summons against Benn, claiming damages of £670 for the loss of his holiday in Antigua.

The first positive response from the Government was the

announcement from Peter Shore's Ministry of Trade (he shared responsibility in this affair with Benn) that the Government would provide an interest-fee loan to help pay back the 100 000 disappointed holiday-makers. But this only provoked the charge from Eldon Griffiths, the Conservative spokesman on Trade, that Labour Ministers were seeking to escape from their responsibility for the crash at the taxpayers' expense, and he formally complained to the Ombudsman. Benn insisted that he did not ask to see the books of the holiday side of Court Line before making his statement in the House of Commons and that the Government was concerned only with the shipbuilding side of Court Line. This was less than convincing because the important part of his statement, indeed the only part which was at issue, concerned the holiday side of Court Line, and if the Government was not concerned about anything but the shipbuilding side, clearly the people who went on and booked their holidays and in consequence lost money following his words of reassurance *were* concerned (as Damon Runyon might say) more than somewhat. In any case, Benn, following his usual course of never apologising (on the whole a wise course for a politician as Disraeli had long ago argued) was determined to brazen it out. He did not mind an enquiry he said with his usual air of injured innocence. He could explain his side of the affair. The less charitably-minded suspected that this was a cover-up to disguise the desperate financial position of Court Line in order that the shipbuilding side of its operation could be annexed by the state.

Of course once official enquiries are set on foot that tends to put an end for the time being to their public airing. Temporarily Benn was therefore off the hook and able to pursue his pre-election propaganda which concentrated on the way Labour, through the efforts of his Ministry, was busy saving workers' jobs by takeovers, of one form or other. Thus, on the first day of the election campaign, he was to be found making a pledge to safeguard the jobs of 16 000 workers belonging to Ferranti, the electronics giant which had been hit by a cash shortage, although on how this would be done he was far from specific. For the few weeks that he was making up his mind Benn kept the company going by guaranteeing further loans from the National Westminster Bank. Then there was Rolls Royce again, which was to receive a £40 million loan to enable it to go into full-scale production of the RB-211 engine, the stratospheric cost of which had landed it in the bankruptcy court under the Heath government.

Benn's Santa Claus act went rather less smoothly at the instrument makers George Kent, in which his Industry Department had a twenty-four per cent stake, when it supported the bid for the company by Sir Arnold Weinstock's giant GEC Group. The workers however (or some of their bosses at George Kent who had, it was said, been indoctrinating them) did not fancy Weinstock taking over as they feared he might make some of them redundant and plumped instead for another bidder, the Swiss firm, Brown Boveri.

This was pretty small beer though, compared with the big state takeover for which Benn was the Labour party's leading crusader. Still, it seems he must have been warned off during the weeks before polling day. Nationalisation was not a popular cause with the workers directly affected; Labour supporters tend to dislike nationalisaton of the business for which they work themselves, although they may not mind it being applied to the firm next door. Benn had said himself on television early in September that 'firms cannot be nationalised without their workers wanting it'. It was something of a rebuff therefore when a week later a National Opinion Poll survey was published which found that only one in eight of those working for private enterprise, when asked if they wanted their firm taken over by the Government, said Yes. And more than half of Labour supporters interviewed were opposed to nationalisation.

It deserves mention here that, a fortnight before the election campaign began, there was the strange but surely

ove: 'I hold the future of
itain in my hands.' The
ergy Minister welcomes the
st North Sea oil ashore,
companied by Frederick
milton, Chairman of the
gyll Consortium.
ess Association Photos)

ght: The candidate.
orking in the basement at
me during the 1976 Labour
dership contest. *(Photograph
Colin Davey, Camera Press)*

The black and white Minister's show. The Energy Minister (top) with miners at Newton-le-Willows colliery, Lancashire, and (bottom) signing the oil participation agreement with (left) Dr Austin Pearce, Chairman of Esso Petroleum and (right) Peter Baxendell, Chairman of Shell UK. *(Central Press Photos)*

revealing incident to which reference was made in Chapter 1, when Benn went out of his way to deny his background and, on the face of it, attempted to create instead a myth of his working class origins. On the evening of 5 September he was taking part in the BBC's *Nationwide* programme, and there was a debate on nationalisation. In this he said quite gratuituously, 'If I go back over my life I was an Aircraftsman, Second Class, for a couple of years and then I worked as a salesman.' This appears to contradict *Who's Who* which recorded that his service career from 1943 to 1946 he was a Pilot Officer in the RAF from 1943 to 1945, and a Sub-Lieutenant in the Fleet Air Arm for the year after. The time he worked as a salesman was for the family business of Benn Brothers, built up by his uncle Ernest, who would certainly not have approved of this posturing in the guise of a common man. One of those who served with Benn, after he had seen the programme, said — surely with remarkable self-restraint — 'Those of us who were aircrew were proud of it'. The truth of the matter was that Benn was during most of his time in the service the conventional officer type.

Benn's last contribution to the Cabinet's transactions, before the election campaign finally got under way, was to hamstring relations with the Common Market. The question arose about whether Britain could give aid to industry free of Brussels control. He forced this question into full Cabinet and managed to achieve what he wanted — open disagreement with the foreign secretary, Mr Callaghan. The clash was over Benn's refusal to allow the Commission to have British working documents effecting State aids like the Regional Employment Premium, a lame duck subsidy on which Brussels had generally frowned. Benn had tried to insist to the Community working party on the matter that Britain would accept no common system of state aids in the EEC which did not leave the last words over British aids to Parliament.

For the moment it was his last essay in trouble-making because in the election itself, as in the preceding one in

February, he was pretty well kept under wraps. At Bristol his agent, Mr Ennis Harris, told reporters, 'No news conference or interviews for the duration of the election'. He went on to say, 'We are rather fed up with the press'. In this he was only echoing Harold Wilson's hostility to the newspapers when he, early in the election, claimed that they were preparing a smear campaign against Labour, and hinted darkly that at the right time his evidence would be produced. In fact it was the Walter Mitty in him coming out again and no evidence was produced either during the campaign or later. It was not only a matter of follow-my-leader though. Wilson was evidently anxious not to lose the large lead which all the polls showed him to possess by making too much noise or stirring things up: he wanted to start in a low key and to stay there, and the suggestion that the press was going to smear him was an attempt to forestall any newspaper's essay in raising the temperature to the point where passions and the election might run out of his control. Miss Nora Beloff of the *Observer,* a much more clued-up political correspondent than she was often given credit for, had an article at the end of the first week suggesting that Wilson would be shifting Benn away from the Department of Industry in order to revive business confidence which, at this stage, was in a state of near collapse. Partly this was a matter of sugaring the pill, but there was also a real difference between Benn and his Cabinet colleagues in that they did not accept his radical view that the impending business crisis should be used as Britain's opportunity for a great leap into socialism. He expressed this view to the party's National Executive on 25 July, that the 'system' (which they interpreted to mean both capitalism and parliamentary government) was collapsing and that this was the time for the Labour party to declare itself for the emergence of a new socialist society. In contrast to this point of view, Wilson and Healey were arch Conservatives. They might pay oral tribute to the distant ideals of a socialist utopia, but their aim was to win the election in the here and now (or the there and then) and if this meant tinkering with the economic system to make it work better, if it meant making concessions to capitalist industry to allow inflationary accounting, or reducing corporation tax or making the price code more flexible, why, God bless their souls, that was what they would do. They were not going to kill the golden goose or even threaten to if it meant dishing their golden opportunity of a decent majority. Should Benn insist on trying to pursue his visionary dreams, he could go and do this as most prophets are obliged to — in the wilderness.

Benn was thus pushed off into the nearest thing to purdah that a general election would permit. He went through his usual routine of speaking around the constituency sitting legs a-dangling on the roof of his rusty Nash Rambler and giving out the old message reduced to puerile simplicity about British private industry failing the nation in not investing enough, calling for more investment from the state and boiling the choice down to Labour with full employment or the Tories and slump. Otherwise he displayed his common man image through his scruffy attire — the fur-collared anorak, the baggy trousers, the large yellow rosette and the unpolished leather boots, and with his election placard propped against an old kitchen stool. This proletarian idyll was more than slightly damaged by the news of a bequest of 172 000 (other reports said £290 000) from his wife Caroline's American mother, Mrs Anne Hamill. As the *Daily Express* William Hickey column gleefully put it, 'Thanks to professional advice on tax avoidance, Mrs Hamill was smart enough to ensure that her dollars would not end up in the British Treasury. Labour's nationalise-and-be-damned Mr Benn — despiser of inherited wealth — cannot even give it away because in Mrs Hamill's will the money is in trust for the Benns' four children'.

Benn did not seek the limelight: even when attacked by Lord Robens as an 'academic revolutionary', he just turned the other cheek. There was one incident it is true which almost got him back into the publicity big time, when he went down to speak in Devon and gave a solemn warning that the Arab sheikhs would be ready to strike a deal with Tories and Liberals to buy the nationalised yard at Appledore, Devon. This prompted Jeremy Thorpe to accuse him of whipping up anti-Arab feeling, which was almost as much of a flight of fancy as the speech itself. Still the whole episode was too bizarre to make a *cause célèbre*. It was really an excess of zeal on Benn's part in pursuing his current monomania about preserving jobs, in this case for saving 700 jobs from the scheming Arabs, which came within hailing distance of trouble with the Race Relations Board and all the rich comedy that that might have afforded.

Labour *was* successful in keeping the temperature down. The usual rule worked, that if a party wins power by a small majority it will increase that majority in another election soon afterwards. Labour thus found themselves with an effective margin of 43 seats over the Conservatives (whose ranks included the speaker), but an overall majority of only four after counting all the other parties. Benn's majority over his Conservative opponent at Bristol South-East rose from 14 per cent to a comfortable 17.7 per cent.

9

EUROPE'S LITTLE ENGLANDER

1974~5

Following Labour's victory in the October general election of 1974, Benn returned with new zest to the interventionist policies left in suspension during the campaign. Within hours of knowing that Labour was back in office, the Cabinet Office was in contact with the Department of Industry, arranging for civil servants to speed up the drafting of the Industry Bill.

There was plenty of scope for intervention in specific firms too. The end of October saw Benn engaged in talks about coming to the aid of the leading tool maker, Alfred Herbert. Again, what interested Benn in particular was the importance of the firm as an employer in the West Midlands. A few days later a workers' co-operative at the bankrupt Kirkby factory received £3.9 million — equivalent to £4000 per worker. He also announced a further £8 million for the Meriden motor cycle co-operative on top of the £4.95 million given earlier in the year. It now seemed that Benn had been provided with a

key to the Mint. As *The Sunday Times* put it, 'Where two or
three shop stewards are gathered together in a bankrupt firm
they have only to knock on Mr Benn's door and millions of
pounds of taxpayers' money is given away — Mr Benn has
been allowed, or so it seems, to set himself up as the Sugar
Daddy of the shop stewards.'

There were no published criteria for aiding these
companies any more than any others. They were helped on
the arbitrary basis of Benn's fancy. That is no exaggeration
because he certainly ignored time after time the advice of his
experts on the Industrial Development Advisory Board,
indeed, in January 1975 Mr Peter Carey, second Permanent
Secretary to the Department, put on record his official
objection to the Kirkby decision. It was no wonder that in
some of these cases the less charitably minded should look for
other than purely altruistic reasons. In the case of Kirkby for
instance, could it be because it was situated on the borders of
the Prime Minister's constituency in Huyton? Probably what
weighed heavily with Benn in that instance though was the
workers' militancy, especially the way they claimed they were
able to force the receiver to sign a declaration that he would
not make anybody redundant. This was just the sort of
democracy welling up from below that Benn tended to go all
dewy-eyed and mystical about. It was the same kind of story
as at Upper Clyde and likely to have the same effect of
fortifying workers in the belief that their troubles were to be
solved not by raised productivity — which in many cases
merely meant dropping restrictions of their own devising —
but by sit-ins and work-ins. In this way, and as a sort of
virility award, they would attract the fairy godmother
attentions of the Department of Industry.

Benn's benevolence had its limits all the same, perhaps one
limit being reluctance to let anyone else infringe his
monopoly of industrial do-gooding. In mid-November it was
reported that he personally stopped the studies which the
European Community was making of the industrial and
regional problems of South Wales. These studies were meant

to be the first steps towards establishing an EEC aid fund to help redundant Welsh steelworkers and miners. The decision was surely not unconnected with his hostility to the European Community and all its works.

He was also at this time, despite the horrifying example of how costs can escalate out of all relation to estimates, as in the case of Concorde, urging Hawker Siddeley to go on with its HS-146 aircraft even though it was against his official advice and ignored the fears of the company that (like the RB-211 engine in the case of Rolls Royce) it might make losses large enough to endanger its very survival.

The biggest fish of all however was British Leyland, the only remaining major British car manufacturer. Plagued more than most by strikes and stoppages which cost it between £20 and £30 million in the year ending March 1974, it ran into a severe shortage of cash. Altogether Leyland needed £70 million working capital and a further £200 million for its investment programme. Benn appointed a team of investigators under Sir Don Ryder to look into Leyland's troubles. In his brief statement to the Commons in mid-December, Benn indicated his intention of using the crisis in the motor industry to further his theories about public ownership. One effect of his interest was, as always, to encourage an inflationary wage claim — in the Leyland case of £16 a week. As soon as workers in such a situation got it into their heads that the Government would pay out any amount of the taxpayers' money in order to protect their jobs the restraint of economic realities was to a great extent removed. The situation that then necessarily developed all too easily was that state money, provided for an investment programme and intended to boost productivity, was simply swallowed up by higher wages which were seen to be the reward of militancy. It was a policy which superficially seemed compassionate towards the workers but it was a proxy compassion exercised on behalf of taxpayers subjected as a result to increasing coercion. Putting it another way, as consumers they were being forced to surrender a part of their income to maintain activities which voluntarily they would not have supported.

To all intents and purposes Benn was now riding high. He had the job he wanted since it was most directly concerned with bringing about that irreversible shift in wealth and power, through nationalisation and interventionism, which he had in the period of opposition so passionately claimed as his prime objective. In fact this was the stage at which he was already starting on the course which was to lead to his removal from his department to one considered less at the centre of policy-making. This was for two reasons. One was that he tended to overreach himself and his utterances sounded too shrill and extremist which was worrying for his Cabinet colleagues who were less interested in revolution than in re-election next time, and Benn's antics were arousing more and more opposition. Another was that he aggravated this unpopularity with his colleagues by his campaign to take Britain out of the Common Market in 1975, because the senior figures in the Cabinet had by now decided that membership, if on slightly revised terms, was essential.

Benn opened that campaign at the end of December 1974 when he made a speech to his constituents in which he declared that the overwhelming objection to membership was that it would mean 'the end of Britain as a completely self-governing nation and the end of our democratically-elected parliament as the supreme law making body in the United Kingdom'. This speech was circulated to most of the other Cabinet Ministers because there was to be a meeting of Ministers in the New Year to consider Common Market policy. It infuriated Callaghan (who was responsible for the renegotiation of terms) because it included the remark that renegotiation was a side issue.

This was only the opening shot in a campaign which was to hot up later as the referendum approached. Meantime he was throwing himself with more energy than ever and with increasingly irritant effect upon an ever wider circle. One Minister, who called at the Department, was greeted by the voice of Benn singing the *Red Flag*. On arrival in his colleague's room, the Minister found on his wall not a tasteful Gainsborough or Reynolds but a huge trades union banner. To some of his working class colleagues this was the sign of a man over-compensating for his aristocratic origins. It was also part of a pose of not being as other Ministers were, but a man of the people whose appeal was over the heads of his colleagues in Cabinet and Commons to the rank and file of the Labour movement in the country at large. One eminent commentator reacted favourably however, namely Paul Johnson, the former *New Statesman* editor whose eulogy of Benn in an article in the *Daily Telegraph* of all places reads particularly strangely today in the light of the passionate and very effective anti-Labour diatribes in which Johnson has since indulged. In this particular article, which was every bit as fanciful as his subject, he depicted the Britain that Benn was fighting against as 'a decaying Ruritania full of bright uniforms and unpaid tailors' bills' and held up Benn as a paragon — 'the best kind of clean-living Englishman'. He even managed to conclude, 'Yet we know in our hearts — do we not? — that Mr Benn is probably right?'. The same thing was said more affirmatively by the posters supporting the ill-fated Goldwater for US President. 'You know in your heart he is right', they asserted from every hoarding and prompted the sneering and devastating response from the Democratic camp, 'In your guts you know he's nuts'.

Benn's industrial advisers too were starting to protest noisily against their advice being ignored. Mr Peter Carey, Second Permanent Secretary to the Department of Industry, and the accounting officer responsible for Industry Act expenditure, was reported in January as having expressed his reservations over Benn's Kirkby scheme in a memorandum which could eventually attract the beady eyes of the Public Accounts Committee. Benn's Advisory Board, headed by Robert Clark, the merchant banker, was also known to have raised objections to the Kirkby, Meridan and *Scottish Daily Express* co-operatives as well as to the aid to Aston Martin's

Lagonda, and it was revealed at this time that the Board also had a difference of view with Benn over the method of giving aid to the machine-tool maker, Alfred Herbert, though the details which were confidential were not reported. Other experts, not ideologists by any means, like James Ensor of *The Financial Times,* were writing warning articles about Benn's wayward support for dicey firms. One Ensor article questioned Benn's aid to the lorry maker Fodens, which had high production costs, a tenuous European deals network and was operating in an industry which suffered from severe over-capacity and at a time when bigger firms, like Berliet, could not survive independently. The dangers of subsidising firms as a sort of reward for the militancy of the work force, which seemed to be Benn's only abiding principle, was driven home by the general manager of Kuwait Shipping after a launching at the Govan Yard on the Upper Clyde: 'We are concerned at the steadily increasing length of delivery time after the contract date, and no amount of monetary penalties we may be paid will compensate us for the loss of revenue and the interference with our commercial development.'

Such criticism however left Benn unmoved. Indeed, his appointment just after the New Year as Chairman of the Labour party's influential home policy committee gave him the opportunity to intensify the pressure for nationalisaiton. Just over a month later, his committee sent a delegation to talk to Ministers to 'remind them of party policy in the area of public ownership' and in particular to warn them against selling Burmah Oil's 20.5 per cent stake in British Petroleum which at that time was being held by the Bank of England. It recommended instead that BP (in which the Government had long had a controlling share) should henceforth be regarded and treated as part of the public sector. Further, it recommended that the Government should take 'a direct stake in Burmah Oil and a substantial one at that'. This was seen as a defiant reaction to the Prime Minister's speech the previous Friday when Mr Wilson had tried to reassure British industry that a Cabinet committee and not the Industry

Secretary would be really responsible for taking decisions on
state takeovers under the new Industry Bill. After Benn had
handed over the chair of the home policy committee to Ian
Mikardo, the committee went on to approve a motion
deploring the Prime Minister's announcement that senior
civil servants, top service officers and judges were to receive
substantial rises in pay.

This was just a week before Benn's Industry Bill came
before the House of Commons. The Bill was designed to
bring about the regeneration of British Industry by
discretionary government action, that is more state control
and the replacement of the businessman by the bureaucrat.
The heart of the Bill was Clause 6, which gave Benn the
power through the agency of the National Enterprise Board
to do anything he liked. In other words Benn was to become
industrial dictator. The NEB was to have £700 million to start
with, rising to £1000 million. In addition, Benn had the
further £550 million (£125 million already used) under Clause
8 of Industry Act of 1972, and unlimited resources under
Clause 7 of that Act. With all these funds available, Benn
would be able to take over and invest to his heart's content.
So, despite all Wilson's assurances to the CBI that they had
nothing to worry about and that Benn was under control, if
the Bill was anything to go by, industry's viewpoints had been
totally ignored. The strong Cabinet committee which Wilson
had promised would exercise a moderating influence had
evidently had no effect on its drafting. Again, the
appointment of Sir Don Ryder — a well-know industrialist as
Chairman of the NEB and another bid by Wilson to reassure
industry — meant little because under the Bill Sir Don was
Benn's poodle.

The most important follow-up to the Bill was the decision
of the Government to take a majority shareholding in British
Leyland in April 1975. The big expense however was
government backing to the Ryder plan for the investment of
£1500 million in British Leyland's development. The same
attitude informed or rather misinformed Benn's attitude to

the steel industry and led to his quarrel with Sir Monty Finniston, the Chairman of British Steel, who wanted to reduce the manning scales, which by international standards were scandalously high and uncompetitive. This meant shutting down inefficient works like that at Shotton. Benn's view was that the men must stay in their jobs. As a matter of principle or dogma, he put the blame never on the striking workers but always on head management, who were responsible for chronic lack of investment. Those who pointed out that industry was only going to invest if it had profits to invest and would only have the will to invest if it saw the prospect of profitability, he simply dismissed with the triumphant assertion that this just showed that regeneration of industry could never come about under a capitalist free market system. To this there was a succinct riposte from Sir Keith Joseph in a speech he made at the Kingston upon Thames Polytechnic 'The Government has starved industry — that is all governments — shackled industry and then complained that it is not performing as well as in countries like West Germany, Switzerland and Japan, where profits are honoured in their own country.'

Benn was more convincing in an article published in *Trade and Industry* on 4 April 1974, in which he pointed to the relatively rapid decline of employment in the manufacturing sector and concluded that if things were left alone we were heading towards the deindustrialisation of Britain. The only hope was to double investment in manufacturing, through drastic state action. As it turned out, the figures on which he based this forecast were twice as alarming as the ones used the the Department of Employment a month later (the 1971-81 estimate was a drop of 530 000 manufacturing jobs, not 1 200 000). Of course, one must always be on the lookout for major changes of trend which threaten to create large-scale unemployment, but in fact there has for over a century been a trend for the service sector to grow faster than the manufacturing. In times past both services and manufacturing grew at the expense of agriculture, but more recently services have been taking labour from industry. This is a trend to be found all over the industrialised world and leads towards what Daniel Bell has christened the *Post Industrial Society*. Nevertheless, there is reason to believe that in Britain in recent years this shift has been occurring too fast for comfort, but not in a form which gives much comfort to the theories of Benn either. The main worry highlighted by Bacon and Eltis in *Britain's Economic Problem* (Methuen, 1976) is that, as a result of the growth of government spending, much of the rise in service employment has been in the unproductive public sector. Besides, Benn's recipe for the problem — more state directed investment — missed the point completely since at very high levels of government expenditure, the direction of investment into industries of Whitehall's choice tends to be financed from resources taken away from those firms in the private sector which are still profitable. Further, Benn-style investment, as experience showed in the many examples quoted here, generally went not to profitable firms but those which were going bankrupt often due to their militant work force who then attracted the sympathetic attention of Benn's department by a sit-in, especially if this were combined with a declaration that they were forming a workers' co-operative. This was the real de-industrialisation of Britain — the throwing of good money after bad, the propping up of declining industries, the rewarding of indifferent management and trade union militants defending restrictive practices to the last picket line and the keeping of an ever-growing burden of tax and bureaucratic meddling on the shrinking part of the private sector which continued to make profits.

The Benn analysis was not however accepted by the rest of the Cabinet, and in particular by Denis Healey, the Chancellor of the Exchequer, who said at the Mansion House on 26 March 1975:

'Investment overall in Britain as a percentage of national output has not been very different from

some of our competitors. The real problem is that
we have failed to direct our investment as wisely as
many other countries; and too often we have failed
to make use of it when it has taken place. The fact
is that we have unused capacity in our economy
today which could increase productivity in a single
year as much as we could hope to achieve from
increased investment over a decade.'

The reference to unused capacity was very relevant: to take
just one example, there were already valuable machines in
newspaper offices in Fleet Street incorporating the new
photographic type-setting technology, which were rusting
unused because of the refusal of the printers and compositors
to let them be operated.

Unfortunately the fallacies of Bennery went marching on.
At the end of April, in a paper to the Labour party's
industrial policy committee, he urged that insurance
companies, pension funds and other institutions should be
compelled to channel some of their new money into
government approved investment schemes. This was where
the extra £3000 million to boost manufacturing investment
was to come from! Then the aircraft and shipbuilding
industries were to be nationalised. Yet shipbuilding
illustrated perfectly the fallacy of the investment as a cure-all
approach, because the already nationalised shipbuilding
yards of Belfast which the government had been shoring up
for years were actually very well-equipped but were still
taking twice as long to build a ship as in other countries where
the equipment was no better. As for the aircraft industry, *The
Economist* pointed out that Benn had been unable to come
up with anything to suggest that nationalisation would
improve its performance. On the contrary, it feared that the
most likely effect would be that Benn would go ahead with
Hawker Siddeley's HS-146, which nobody would want to buy
in the foreseeable future. There was a sort of crazy logic
about all this: only nationalised industries (or private firms

with total government backing, as with Concorde) would invest without qualms in developing a dud product. Therefore it was necessary to extend public ownership in order to carry out his lame duck or dead duck investment programme. It was all reminiscent of the Soviet approach to economic policy — and Benn was showing increasing admiration and warmth towards the regimes in the Soviet bloc — with their emphasis on a high ratio of capital ivestment in heavy industry, for which there was always demand because of the big armaments programme — but it significantly coincided with a dreadfully low standard of living, and a general frustration and discontent in the community which, in Russia, has expressed itself in an appalling degree of alcoholism, especially among the young.

Admittedly thus far it was just Benn theorising and it was possible to argue that Benn was less dangerous in practice than he looked. Enoch Powell for instance said in a speech to a London business conference that the Industry Bill was a paper tiger, that it was not a nationalisation act and advised against campaigns against Wedgwood Benn — 'Don't holler until you're hurt,' he said. The main thing he advised was not to be bullied into voluntary co-operation agreements and not to seek aid from the NEB. The positive side of this advice was sound and much needed, because business men tend to be rather naive about politics and are too easily tricked or cajoled by a past master of these arts, like Benn, into doing what he wants. But the Act, as we have seen, *did* give considerable nationalising powers to the NEB and if firms only hollered when they were hurt, it might be too late. Perhaps in the event, external restraints like the balance of payments, and the need to behave in a manner acceptable to our international creditors, especially the International Monetary Fund, would emasculate the Act in its immediate effects, but that was no reason to go easy on opposing it. For one of the more obvious lessons of history is that if discretionary powers are there, sooner or later somebody will use them. The eternal vigilance, which is notoriously the price of democracy, needs to be exercised at the embryo stage, in order, as it were, to nip the budding tyranny in the bud. It is hard to believe however that Powell, who rarely says anything without a purpose, was altogether uninfluenced in these comments by his main preoccupation which was opposition to continued membership of the Common Market and in this endeavour Benn was his ally who was best shielded from the calumny of the business community.

It was a triumph for the persistent advocacy of Benn that Labour decided that a referendum on whether Britain should remain in the Common Market would actually take place in early June 1975. Admittedly when Benn had first put the referendum idea forward it was as a pro marketeer at the time when he was supporting the typical Wilson idea that there should be a European technological Community, the heat of which would hopefully be more white than his own purely British version. Benn had further said it was the only way to beat the multinationals. Why had he changed his tune since then? Probably for tactical reasons. It is hard to believe that he was unaware of the advantages it offered in the power struggle inside the Labour party. In opposing membership of the Community, Benn was probably appealing to the Labour grass roots, certainly to the Labour Left and to most of the union leaders. Handled properly, here was an issue which could be used to gain control of the Labour party by identifying Wilson and his supporters with a policy unpopular within the movement. Others understood this too. In March, at the first anti-market rally after the terms of renegotiation were announced, Benn was in attendance and so was Peter Shore, but they were the only two of the seven Cabinet ministers who had voted in the Commons against the renegotiated terms. His Deputy Industry Minister and fellow member of the Left, Eric Heffer, resigned over the terms, and when Wilson was slow to replace him it was said by cynics that the reason was that he wanted to make Benn work harder.

A special conference was called by the Labour party to

discuss terms of entry and Benn told a rally in Central Hall, Westminster: 'It is now clear that the whole campaign for British withdrawal from the Common Market has got to be led and organised by the British Labour Movement.' This appeal seems to have been heard by the special conference which duly voted two to one in favour of the (left-wing) National Executive's recommendation that Britain should leave the Common Market. Following this there was a move by certain Labour backbenchers to 'Fire Tony Benn'. But Wilson was not going to do that while the referendum campaign was going on, especially when the Tories were calling for his head on a platter. But Benn had to put up with a wigging from Ron Hayward — the Labour party General Secretary (and one who owed his appointment to Benn's casting vote) — for daring to suggest that the party apparatus should be used to propogate the views of the anti-Europe Left.

Benn's response was to grow still wilder in his accusations. He was soon claiming that membership had already cost Britain half a million jobs because unemployment was an EEC disease. This evoked the wrath of one ministerial colleague after another. Tony Crosland, the Environmental Minister said that Benn had contradicted himself. If unemployment was, as he said, an EEC disease, how could Benn reconcile this with his earlier statement that, as a result of the Treaty of Rome, jobs were being exported to the continent at the expense of the British workers? Less elegantly but more forcefully, Robert Mellish, Labour's Chief Whip, denounced Benn's assertions as 'downright lies'. A few days later Denis Healey, Chancellor of the Exchequer, joined the attack on Benn, saying that those who sought foreign scapegoats for our troubles were escaping into a cocoon of myth and fantasy. The reason for the unemployment, he said, was 'that Britain was not producing enough goods, which either foreigners or Britons wanted, at a price they could afford'. Next to take the stump was Harold Wilson himself. Far from membership of the Common

Market losing jobs, he said, it actually led to the creation of
more jobs; large American companies seeking a base for
operations in Europe would come to Britain, but only if she
were a member of the European Community. There were also
at least eighty EEC companies which had decided to set up in
Britain since entry. On the same day, Roy Jenkins entered the
lists and scathingly said he could not longer take Benn
seriously as an economic minister. He went on:

> 'It is this technique in which you just think of a
> number and double it, and if challenged — and Mr
> Benn has been challenged by people in great
> authority, like the Prime Minister, the Chancellor
> of the Exchequer and the Foreign Secretary — you
> pretend that you have not been challenged and
> react by thinking up some new claim.'

The referendum was imminent and there were plans for a
television debate just before the poll. The idea was to have
the antis' opening speech by Enoch Powell and the winding-
up speech by Benn. They were to be opposed by Heath and
Jenkins. This was put in some confusion by Benn's refusal to
sit next to Enoch. Evidently he did not want to be publicly
identified with him. That did not stop Enoch defending Benn
a few days later when he said that such firms as British
Leyland and Ferranti 'couldn't see more than a year ahead
and then blamed Mr Wedgwood Benn'. At the same time
Benn was defended — more usefully from the point of view
of support within the party — by Ron Hayward, the party
General Secretary, who said in effect 'Sack Benn at your
peril' and warned the Prime Minister that Benn was only
doing his job. This counsel to Wilson was in response to the
Prime Minister's threat earlier in an interview that Ministers
vociferously opposed to the Common Market could expect to
be moved from departments dealing regularly with the
Community after a 'Yes' vote.

That this sort of decision should have to be considered was a curious twist of fate because the Common Market had not been a popular cause even such a short time ago as the Labour party conference. What happened was that Wilson and most of the senior Ministers had campaigned for remaining in the Community on the terms negotiated while the Conservatives too were campaigning officially for remaining in. Consequently public opinion changed round, and the result was a large majority in favour. So in the event the power of the Left and the cohorts of unionism was revealed to be much smaller than anyone had imagined. When it came to it, the· British people would accept responsible leadership and were neither as disorientated nor as ungovernable as some pessimists were suggesting.

Benn himself took what was after all a considerable personal defeat very well. 'I have just been in receipt of a very big message from the British people. I read it loud and clear,' he said at an impromptu press conference in the front garden of his London house. He continued:

> 'It is clear that by an overwhelming majority, the British people have voted to stay in, and I am sure that everybody would want to accept that. That has been the principle of all of us who have advocated the referendum.'

Asked about the future of the anti-EEC campaign, he said,

> 'I have always said the referendum would be binding. There will be discussions about our relationship, but clearly the decision of the referendum will be binding on Parliament. There can be no going back.'

Did this mean that Benn was for the chop? There were plenty who would have liked to see him go, including at this stage probably Wilson himself, but it would not have been Wilson's style. Wilson's consistent aim was to make Labour a united party, united not so much on policy as on a resolve to govern, or at any rate to hold office. To dismiss Benn would have made Wilson a prisoner of the Social Democrats, whereas his art had always been to ride all the factions of the party and keep them in balance. Besides, even if his inclination had been to dismiss Benn at this point, he would have been dissuaded by his tiny majority. The last thing he wanted was to have Benn, who had been made more of a national figure than ever by the referendum campaign, putting himself at the head of a group bent on denying Denis Healey his expenditure cuts, for that would bring his so-called economic strategy down about his ears. Even so, apart from the point that Wilson had himself made threats about shifting Ministers who were anti-EEC from posts where they would have frequent dealings with the European Community, there was the fact that he had also committed himself in conversations with various political correspondents to 'doing something' about Benn. Besides, the atmosphere was right for taking Benn down a peg. An analysis of the referendum results suggested that, as in the 1970 general election campaign, Benn had brought out the opposition. The appropriate thing was to shift him with a slight element of demotion. So out went Benn from Industry and away to Energy — though from the point of view of reducing Benn's dealings with Brussels this was, if anything, a change for the worse. Still, it was just enough of a move down the Ministerial ladder not to provoke Benn's resignation. The Tribune Group sent a letter of protest, but even that was a fiasco since only thirty out of the eighty members attended the meeting which approved the letter and Leslie Huckfield, a prominent member of the group, said it was the sort of thing which would give the group a permanent label of the 'looney Left'. Harold Wilson anyway brushed the letter aside as 'regrettably hysterical in tone and inaccurate in content'. This was the rather inglorious finale to Benn's premature bid for power. Nevertheless, he was still in office and his eager spirit already saw exciting possibilities in his new post.

10

MR. ENERGY
IN POWER
1975~8

If Harold Wilson thought that he had pushed Benn into the sidelines by moving him from the exciting, controversial front line Ministry of Industry to the outer Siberia of the Ministry of Energy, he was wrong. For Benn arrived just in time to turn on the first supplies of North Sea oil. Accordingly on 18 June 1975, he travelled up the Thames on a Russian-built hydrofoil to BP's oil refinery on the Isle of Grain, where he turned the control valve to set the oil flowing. Never one to be at a loss for a few choice words, he declared exuberantly, 'This is far more significant and historic for Britain than a moonshot. This is a day of national celebration. We will in time be one of the top ten oil producers in the world.' Then, holding a bottle of crude oil aloft, he asserted, 'I hold the future of Britain in my hands'. He went on to demand for the British people 'a full and fair return' without it apparently occurring to him that the people who ought in the first place to merit some just reward for their labours were those who took the risks, and that if the British people, as represented by Benn, were too greedy, the risk takers might be gone and much of the oil, or at least the prospect of its further development, with them. No matter: if North Sea oil was to be a bonanza for the British people, it was also likely to be a bonus for Benn, and the more the oil flowed, the more kudos would come to him, almost as if he were producing the stuff himself. And while there was at this time almost universal gloom on the economic front, it fell to Benn, the congenital optimist, to announce the good news about the riches in store, just waiting to be picked off Britain's generous portion of the continental shelf.

Though demoted from industrial overlord to middle rank Cabinet Minister, he was still a kind of overlord of all the traditional energy industries like coal, electricity, gas and oil, as well as the newer, trendier ones like atomic energy and those still in their infancy, like thermal, tidal, wind and solar power. Besides, in contrast to Industry where his role was grandiose, pontifical, rhetorical, inspirational, and sporadically interventionist, the task in Energy was more specific, executive and down to earth. Moreover, it was a job which, as things turned out, Benn was fated to hold not only up to Harold Wilson's retirement from Number 10, but also during the tenure of Callaghan, his successor. Therefore his purely departmental career should be examined in detail.

Benn's most immediate concern on taking over Energy was to establish control over newly gushing North Sea oil so that it should be milked of as much revenue as possible. An early priority was to establish an oil board to overlook the industry in the right, or rather the left, spirit. So Benn proceeded to appoint three directors old enough to draw their pensions, Lord Kearton, the Chairman, aged 65, Lord Balogh, Deputy Chairman, aged 70 and Lord Briginshaw, aged 67. None had any oil industry experience but at least they were all the Prime Minister's friends. A major aim of Labour policy at this time was to obtain a fifty-one per cent stake in the industry and at first there appeared to be no difficulty about this as Healey's fiscal squeeze on private business was making for hard times even among the corporate giants. One such was Burmah Oil, which had the special problem of having too many tankers laid up. Benn was therefore able to negotiate for Burmah Oil's stake in two of the biggest North Sea oilfields at a bargain basement price because the company was struggling to get out of debt. In the end though the other oil companies proved less easy to push around, and besides the financial resources simply were not available for the state to buy its way in. So Harold Lever, then Chancellor of the Duchy of Lancaster and the Government's chief negotiator, worked out a curious face-saving formula by which the British National Oil Corporation (BNOC) generally took fifty-one per cent of the oil produced from the companies at market prices (which was then resold to the companies) instead of a majority shareholding. Even so, the harmless-sounding Petroleum and Submarine Pipelines Act, which received Royal Assent in November 1975, gave the Government sweeping powers of control over North Sea oil. Benn could therefore be content that the instrument was at hand whenever the time looked ripe to use it — that was, when it was no longer so necessary to butter up the oil companies. In the meantime, he relied on the steady pressure he was able to exert on them through his control over production licences. As early as September 1975 for example, he said that the licences would be issued on condition that the companies concerned bought more oil rigs in Britain and were co-operative among other things in helping the development of trades union organisations. The method of making the oil companies conform was to have them sign participation agreements with the BNOC and a growing number of companies big and small did so.

The danger with bodies like the BNOC which possess such large reserve discretionary powers is that, sooner or later they will tend to use them. Leaving aside the traditional constitutional concern about discretionary power, which even apart from tending in the long run to corrupt, can also in the short term fall into the wrong hands, there is the far from negligible question of economic efficiency: what was the BNOC supposed to do? Its functions were by no means clear.

Benn evidently thought of it as a potential state oil company, but what was the point when the Government already owned half of British Petroleum? The most convincing view is that Benn wanted BNOC in the first place to keep a check on the multinational companies (of which he had an inordinate suspicion, especially regarding their ability to evade tax) and, in the second place as a means of creating jobs, an obsession of Benn's related to his general populist approach to economic policy. That called for the creation of jobs not only for the (somewhat ageing) boys — like Balogh and Briginshaw — but jobs in British yards making oilrigs, or jobs in British oil refineries — which was the point of the options to buy fifty-one per cent of the crude produced because when necessary it could be steered into British refineries instead of American ones. If so, it was an extremely cumbersome and bureaucratic method of achieving what could be just as easily brought about by the British refineries simply buying the oil from the companies at the market price. No wonder some business men dubbed BNOC 'British Nonsense Over Crude'.

The actual size of the North Sea oil output probably surpassed the expectations even of Benn, the eternal optimist, who kept on bobbing up with new estimates of the scale of it all. Thus in November 1975 he announced that the North Sea would yield £3000 million a year in the 1980s. By April 1977 he was saying that the Exchequer would by that time be extracting £4250 million a year, and he added that the value of Britain's North Sea oil and gas reserves was a staggering £300 billion. How was all this money to be used? That was the 'great debate' in which the Labour party has ever since been indulging. The full ramifications of this debate need not concern us here because it has reached out over the whole field of economic policy, but it is instructive to consider Benn's view. The Labour Cabinet was split into two camps — with Benn on one side and Healey, the Chancellor of the Exchequer, on the other. Healey, with Whitehall backing, wanted to use the revenue primarily to cut taxation and repay international debts. Benn preferred to boost public spending on services (though not *the* services) construction and more investment in manufacturing industry. This last industrial investment was to be channelled (surprise! surprise!) through the National Enterprise Board, the nationalised industries and other state bodies. When the trades union and Labour party representatives met in their Liaison Committee in November 1977 to discuss the matter, it was the Benn view that prevailed.

The same urge towards centralisation and the same obsession with creating jobs, with scant regard to costs, appeared in his approach to the Electricity industry. The Plowden report had already recommended in January 1976 that the Central Electricity Generating Board and the Electricity Council should be merged into one body. This however, would have magnified the damage done to the economy whenever blunders were made at the centre. The need of the industry was to be more flexible in meeting the competition of rival fuels and for that, the area boards needed more power. However, Benn's main concern with these area electricity authorities was that he should have the power to appoint their chairmen — a fine example of double-think considering how given he was to condemning the power of patronage in other people — the Prime Minister for instance. For that matter, nobody was ever more anxious to move away from the 'arm's length' relationship between Minister responsible and nationalised industry chiefs (as laid down by Herbert Morrison just after the war), and to make the latter his creatures, obedient to his policy directives, taking instructions meekly from his department's civil servants and deferential to Benn's union friends. The same applied elsewhere in his domain: so it did not take Benn long to tire of Sir Derek Ezra, Chairman of the Coal Board, and in the spring of 1975 it was reported that, without Ezra's knowledge, he had been asking the miners to find a replacement. Nor was this unprecedented since, when Postmaster General, he sought union advice before re-appointing Sir William Rylands as Post Office head. Significantly, Benn's sympathies were strongly with the Plowden merger but he was also, as we shall see, much given to delaying decisions, especially if there was the least excuse for worker consultation. As a result, the merger did *not* go through because it was one of the schemes to which the Liberal party had objected, and it became one of the few small sacrifices which the Labour government made to keep the Lib/Lab pact going during 1977.

The make-work approach to policy was shown in the long drawn-out decision to order a £600 million power station, Drax B, two years before it was needed. The order went to the Tyneside firm of C.A. Parsons which was faced with 1600 redundancies. From the efficiency point of view the contract should have gone to Arnold Weinstock's General Electric Company, but GEC was not allowed to compete. The fact that Drax B was uneconomic was underlined by the protests of the CEGB management and confirmed by the eventual agreement of the Government to pay the Electricity Board £50 million in compensation for ordering a power station which was uncommercial. Benn was anxious to press on with the order, not only for the work it provided for the plant-makers, but also because Drax B was coal-fired, and the miners wanted it to assure future jobs in the Selby coalfield.

These episodes illustrate the wide range of Benn's energy kingdom, but he could not be content with a pragmatic approach to each of its provinces; though he lacked the genuine philosophic mind, he had a definite yearning for system. Why not then have an overall integrated policy for all forms of energy, the principles of it to be laid down by himself, from the centre? And if it was far from clear what those principles should be, then what an opportunity to promote a discussion among all those involved — economists, planners, managers, workers, from all the different industries, consumers even — all discoursing together, opinions jostling, conflicting, but fruitfully yielding copious information, prodigious insights — especially when encouraged by the Minister presiding in person. So that at the end there would emerge, phoenix-like out of the ashes of debate and the dawning spirit of consensus, an energy plan! Such appears to have been the immaculate conception which Benn's romantic imagination conjured up of the National Energy Conference of 500 experts which he called in June 1976 at London's Church House. What actually happened was that all the participants shouted the odds for their own group. The coal and nuclear power representatives said they must be subsidised to keep going until the 1990s when other fuels ran out. The Electricity men said that cheap gas should be taxed. The Gas men opined that the postulated 1990 energy gap was rot, and then to the astonishment of one and all, Lord Ryder, fresh from the interventionist orgies of the National Enterprise Board, talked as if subsidies were sinful and asked of the proposal to tax gas whether he had come to a mad hatter's tea party! This was one time throughout the conference when Benn did not applaud. Perhaps the future had cast its shadow before since in the following March he was authorising a rise of ten per cent in gas prices which actually broke the Government's own prices code! This decision nicely illustrated how devoid of principle the policy actually was. It was just a matter of which sectional or voting interest could lobby to most effect.

In any case, as George Gale commented at the time in the *Daily Express,* the presumption that the country needed a 'policy' for energy any more than policies for housing, transport, regional development or anything else remotely susceptible to bureaucratic planning and control, was 'both endemic and dangerous'. Why assume that a Minister and a handful of civil servants could produce a more economical, sensible, equitable result than the free play of market forces? Why indeed should anybody believe that the Whitehall experts possessed any special insight into the future after the prize boobs they had made in the past? The Coal Board's notorious plan for coal in 1956 was the all-time classic, for it predicted a coal shortage 'for as far ahead as we can see'.

Next year there was a glut.

One of the troubles with nationalised monopolies is that, in the nature of the case, they cannot rely on market forces to sort out the problems of supply and demand and some politican, or more correctly some civil servant, has to make long-term decisions about how whole industries shall change. The general assumption on which the Labour government has in recent years been working, whether sensible or not, has been that there will be a shortage of conventional energy sources by the 1990s, and that a larger supply of nuclear energy is essential to fill the gap. To simplify a complicated controversy which split the Labour Cabinet, the big choice was between backing a proven American model, the so-called Pressurised Water Reactor (PWR) and the British Advanced Gas-Cooled Reactor (AGR) which was still in its early phase of development. Benn's first inclination was to put off the decision as long as possible. His second was to plump for the British design. In early 1978 Benn announced that two AGRs were going to be built in England and one in Scotland. It looked very like Benn in his technocratic days at Min Tech with his romantic nationalist approach to science-based industries which brought him to believe that home-grown technology is best. In fact there was no reason why Britain should not simply use the American design and pay royalties, which would be a fraction of the total cost. After all, the Royal Navy was already using the PWR reactors in its nuclear submarines. To be nationalistic about technology was, as we have already seen, the way to waste money on projects of the Concorde variety. He had, perhaps, the excuse that buying British was recommended by the twenty-three strong Energy Commission which he set up in October 1977, but then this body, like most of its type, was dominated by producer interests.

In all these areas of his responsibility Benn had been energetic indeed, but not especially swift in making decisions, no doubt partly because his love of debate made it seem better to travel hopefully than to arrive. He had some excuse for delay in that the stagnation of the economy under Labour had led to a falling-off in the demand for energy. Even so, there was a discernible tendency to resort to bodies like the Energy Commission as talking-shops which gave the impression of something being done, but were in fact excuses for putting off controversial decisions.

Much more to his taste were dramatic acts of intervention calculated to bring big electoral returns. There were his decisions in the summer of 1976 to give more time to pensioners to pay their winter fuel bills, and the follow-up, a £25 million subsidy to cut electricity bills for those, seventy per cent of them pensioners, who were receiving supplementary benefits. Well intentioned no doubt but it tended also to make fools of the thrifty honest folk who paid their bills promptly. In the outcome nearly half those eligible did not claim, though no doubt it all helped to put a little shine on Labour's compassionate image at relatively small cost. Then there was Benn's great energy-saving plan coming out just before Christmas 1977, which over a period of four years, was to spend £320 million on saving energy, a typical Bennite feature of which was the free insulation of council houses. There was, equally typically, nothing for owner occupiers, but that did not stop Benn claiming prospective savings in energy costs which his scheme would bring of £700 million in ten years' time, which included the savings achieved by private individuals spending their own money. Similar savings could of course occur simply as a result of private economies stimulated by higher fuel prices. Two months later, the bit now well between his teeth, Benn was putting forward the highly authoritarian suggestion that there should be a ban on the sales of homes which failed to meet national insulation standards. Another milder measure which he actually did carry through was the requirement that new cars for sale should carry a label giving official fuel consumption figures. This was one of his more useful ideas, but the way he did it characteristically involved the creation of a government unit which elaborately tested cars by simulating driving in towns and at two higher speeds, though similar tests were already carried out by independent bodies such as *Motoring Which.*

Of course Benn was not one to allow ministerial labours to absorb him so completely as to make him forget the need to repair and strengthen his links with the party, which was his power base, or more the point, neglect his supporters within the party who were found in the unions and on the Left. This, however, led to constant conflict between him and Harold Wilson, and after the leadership change, between him and Jim Callagham, with the result that Benn's survival in the Cabinet often seemed at stake. Thus in July 1975 he let it be known among left-wing MPs that he was against the Government's economic policy, wanted, like the Tribune Group, to have import controls and strict application of the price code, and was only staying in the Government because he could play a role when Healey's policies failed to work. Soon after this, Benn challenged Wilson with a call for massive state control of industry. 'Labour must exploit the economic crisis as the occasion for change and not the cause for postponing it'. It was a good curtain raiser for that year's party conference where Benn had the satisfaction of topping the poll in the vote for the National Executive, while his cup must have run over when Healey was voted off altogether and replaced by left-wing Eric Heffer. He also helped to reject a demand for nationalisation of 250 firms — even Benn thought that that was going a bit fast — but assured the conference that they were not there to manage capitalism, but to change society. Back in Cabinet he rebelled against Healey's programme of spending cuts, and along with Peter Shore and others led a new attack on the Common Market, only six months after the referendum which was supposed by his own admission to have settled it. On the Home Policy Committee in January 1976 he (the champion of open government) set about suppressing a report by the Transport House Research Department which suggested that the mere maintenance of existing government expenditure would require an across-the-board increase in all taxes of ten per cent. A fortnight later the National Executive earned a reprimand from Wilson for passing a resolution (which plainly reflected Benn's attitude in particular) criticising his administration of the honours system — a point on which, as time was to show, he had reason to be sensitive. In March Benn's constituency Labour party, obviously echoing his own views, published a resolution 'totally opposing' all the cuts in public expenditure and calling for the redirection of the Labour government towards socialist policies. Benn was pushing his luck. He later revealed that during this period he received six notes from Wilson threatening to drop him from the Cabinet for not supporting his policies.

The danger faded however with Wilson's surprise announcement on 16 March 1976 that he was going to resign. There was an immediate race for the leadership. The heavyweight contenders were Callaghan, Jenkins and Foot. After a pause to ponder they were joined by Healey and Crosland, and with neither pause nor pondering by Benn who told Foot (who as a fellow member of the Left may have hoped Benn would stand down in his favour) 'I will stand for election even if I get only one vote, and that my own'. Benn was anxious to stand, not because he thought he could win, but because, by doing so, he established himself as a contender for the next time round. It also gave him a platform for publishing what he stood for, which he was able to do the more freely because he did not aim to win, so did not care about offending some voters, whereas the serious candidates stuck to private lobbying by their friends. Thus Benn alone of the contenders issued a personal manifesto. It demanded more socialism, state-led expansion of the economy, open government, and industrial democracy. In the vote, as a matter of fact, he did quite well with 30 votes, less than Foot with 90, Callaghan with 84, Jenkins with 56, and Healey with 37, but nearly twice as many as his old Oxford tutor, Crosland with 17. In the final ballot Benn supported Foot but Callaghan won decisively with 176 to

Foot's 137.

In his last days before resigning Harold Wilson had had a final fling in exercising his authority. He had put the rebels in their place with a clear Commons vote of confidence on the 11 March, after which three rebellious junior Ministers, including Benn's aide, Joe Ashton, resigned. A fortnight later Wilson placed a gag on Benn, instructing him to stop holding press conferences in his capacity as Chairman of Labour's Home Policy Committee. This did not seem to worry Benn, who was reported the same day to have been on excellent form at Wilson's farewell dinner party — a convivial affair where he had made a speech confessing that eleven years before he had recorded a radio interview not for immediate use which was to be used in an obituary programme on Harold Wilson. When asked what had been the 'late' Prime Minister's greatest shortcoming he had said it was that he had gone straight into a government post, so that he had never been a backbench MP. Now at last, Benn observed, that was to be put right. A day later, however, with equal good humour he was cocking a snook yet again at Wilson and his memorandum about the Cabinet's collective responsibility by announcing that he was backing the call of the National Executive and the TUC for import controls.

A week later Callaghan was in charge and he, in turn, delivered a public rebuke to Benn for not voting for the Government when other left wingers on the National Executive pushed through a vote condemning expenditure cuts. Callaghan plainly was not going to put up with any nonsense and Benn made a conciliatory gesture by publicly endorsing the four and a half per cent pay limit when he spoke to miners' delegates in early May. The heat was off, especially when he made further obeisance winding up a debate about banks and insurance companies, in which he confirmed that the Government had no intention of nationalising them though he covered himself with the qualification that there might well be new commitments when the new manifesto was written. However, he was raising his head again in July, giving his approval in Labour's home policy committee to a document which described Healey's expenditure cuts as 'a grave economic mistake'. Nor did he show up at the National Executive in July to support Cabinet policy when the NEC in fact carried a resolution attacking the cuts.

It is amusing, incidentally, to note how, during the summer recess, Benn was at odds with Industry Secretary, Eric Varley, over the proposal of Toyota to set up a big warehousing and distribution centre to ship their cars into this country at Avonmouth, Bristol. Varley wanted to push the Japanese and their terminal off to some 'assisted' area like Merseyside, but the Japanese would not have it. Apart from being an enthusiast for regional policy, Benn should, as a keen protectionist, have been all for putting a spoke in the wheels of the Japanese, but then there was the further complication that Bristol was his constituency and the terminal would create 400 jobs. Benn knew which side his bread was buttered on, just as he had earlier in the case of Concorde, and he made it clear that he was supporting Toyota for all he was worth.

By September, however, Benn was back towing the line on the big issue of government economies and refusing to support Barbara Castle's motion at the home policy committee which condemned them, and later in the National Executive he voted to help defeat the same motion, also from Barbara Castle. Yet only three days later at Blackpool on conference eve, he was publicly backing the nationalisation of banking and insurance. When Callaghan spoke to the conference he poured cold water on the plans of the Left and even condemned industry planning agreements, on which Benn was known to be keen, as shotgun marriages. Benn was seen to be biting hard on his pipe during this performance, but he could hardly have been dissatisfied with the actual results of the conference, which called for a more extensive socialist programme than that being put forward by the Italian Communist Party. It included among other things the banning of council house sales, removal of tax relief on house mortgages, an end to prescription charges, abolition of private medicine, nationalisation of the drugs industry, repeal of the 1968 and 1971 Immigration Acts, stopping direct elections to the European Parliament, extravagantly upping pensions, nationalisation of banking and insurance, and opposition to cuts in public spending.

The next battle was over the Queen's Speech, their own draft of which the National Executive wanted to submit at an unprecedented meeting to the Cabinet. The draft included demands for an annual wealth tax, nationalisation of all ports, relaxation of immigrant rules and the ending of the charity status of independent schools. The paper was compiled by Geoff Bish, the Labour party's head of research, who worked closely with Benn. At the end of October, the National Executive (Benn having quit before the vote), with the Prime Minister present, actually voted against the Government's economic strategy by thirteen to six.

Less encouraging to Benn was the report in November of a poll of bank employees which showed that they were overwhelmingly opposed to nationalisation. Still, for practical purposes he could afford to ignore them since they possessed no clout where it mattered — in the TUC and on Labour's NEC.

The latter body was improving daily from Benn's point of view, for it next turned its attention to new methods of electing the leader — inevitably meaning that they would call for an extension of the vote beyond the Labour MPs to include the party conference and the Executive. Naturally any such move would greatly improve Benn's chances, given his enormous popularity with the conference and identification with the NEC. At his behest, the Transport House Research Department next produced a plan for reducing the House of Lords to a cipher.

In December Benn was back on the stump, this time in Sunderland, condemning his own government for not letting the British people know the truth and observing that they deserved better than just 'rumours' based on 'guesswork and unofficial briefing'. This was only the prelude to a full scale row over the appointment of the Trotskyite Andy Bevan as Labour party Youth Officer. Callaghan was furious and let it be known that Ministers on the National Executive who voted for Bevan would be sacked. Even so, Benn stuck to his guns and justified Bevan's appointment in a long memorandum published in *The Observer* in which he observed rightly that Marx had played a central role in the thinking of the Labour party — in other words that it was the party of class war. He quoted Andy Bevan approvingly, saying that he stood on the ideas of Marx and Engels, Lenin and Trotsky, 'but not treating their ideas as dogma'. In fact Bevan was a typical hard line Trot who was engaged with others of the so-called Militant Tendency, which employed full-time activists in an effort to take over the Labour party from within and in particular to infiltrate constituency organisations with the object of expelling MPs who would not conform to the lefty line. Bevan was in fact on the Executive Committee of Newham Constituency and had a hand in the plot against the member, Reg Prentice. In any event, the National Executive met on 15 December and decided by fifteen votes to twelve to ratify his appointment, Benn voting with the majority.

New evidence linking Bevan and the other Trotskyists with a systematic plan to oust moderate socialist MPs was produced by Reg Underhill, Labour's National Agent, just after the conference. When this evidence was presented to the National Executive it was first of all ignored and then consigned to the archives of Transport House. All that saw the light of day was a bowdlerised summary which was sent round to the constituency branches, even this accompanied by a note suggesting that it might be false, exaggerated, or sheer fantasy.

Labour's agents next refused to work with Bevan, not on the proper grounds that he was an enemy of democracy working to take over the Labour party, but more ironically because he was not a member of the National Union of

Labour Organisers, which in any case they refused to let him join. As a result, Bevan was suspended indefinitely on full pay, after a three-hour debut in his office in Transport House. The National Executive at its next meeting however confirmed his appointment eighteen to none.

The Left/Right conflict in the Cabinet continued, but it was lightened by at least one flash of humour. Callaghan, at one Cabinet meeting, grew tired of Benn's droning on interminably about some controversial document. 'Tony', said Jim, 'This must stop. You don't know what you're on about. I don't believe you've even read the document. You're talking sheer political prejudice.' 'Prime Minister', replied Benn, 'you're right and I would ask for 100 similar cases to be taken into account.'

Shortly after this, Benn addressed the Press Gallery at a lunch on parliamentary reform and had the nerve to call for a curbing of the power of Prime Ministers. Next month he was off on another tack, writing in the Church of England magazine, *Theology,* of how Marxists were being hounded by the establishment, the press and the police in Britain. The basis of his discourse was a book called *A Marxist View of Jesus* by Dr Machovec, a former philosophy professor at Prague. 'We must now await a similar work of sensitive scholarship by a Christian writing about Marx,' he said. Those who remember the Red Dean and have since witnessed how fast the Church of England and the other denominations have been moving to the left can only suppose that he must have been joking.

Somehow Benn managed to stay in the Cabinet and at the same time indicate to his supporters that he was not in favour of the Government's policies, that he did not accept the terms of the IMF loan, and that public spending should never be cut. In June 1977 he opened up on another front in a speech in which he said that Britain could still leave the Common Market, 'if Parliament and the people decided'. No more talk now of Parliament trembling when the people spoke — as they had two to one in favour of Europe in the referendum two years before. The real row was over direct elections to the European Parliament to which Britain was committed by membership of the Community. When the second reading of the European Assembly Elections Bill came up on 7 July, six cabinet Ministers including Benn and twenty-six junior Ministers voted against. This time, however, he and they were safe, because Callaghan had allowed a free vote. By the time of the party conference, though, this particular line was beginning to look unpromising, especially when Peter Shore told the Fabians at Brighton that the question of British membership had been settled 'for this Parliament at least' by the referendum. The situation looked even bleaker when the TUC meeting at Blackpool the following week threw out an ASTMS-sponsored motion calling for withdrawal. Also at the TUC Conference it just so happened that, while Callaghan was speaking about the need to fight the battle against inflation, Benn was speaking to what the Fabians called a lunch about the opposite need for a socialist strategy to combat unemployment. He said innocently, 'I haven't gone an inch beyond Labour party policy'.

At the Labour conference the following week the National Executive defied Callaghan and insisted on having a debate on the motion that every sitting MP should be reselected before each general election. Obviously with the Andy Bevans of the party increasingly taking over in the constituencies, this would have suited Benn very nicely. In the event, the TUC barons decided not to exact their pound of flesh and not to force the issue with an election pending, so in the conference the motion was rejected.

As autumn turned to winter, there was the usual worry about pay demands and in particular about whether the power workers and the miners would breach the ten per cent pay limit. Both of these groups were unhappy, and both were dealing with Benn. The power men, who wanted cheap electricity and payment for inconvenient shifts, started to work to rule and this led to a number of blackouts. It was Benn's clear duty to speak out in favour of the pay policy, but, though this would have pleased his Cabinet colleagues it would not have gone down well with the Left. So he stayed mum and explained his silence saying that he was active behind the scenes. He should have given some moral support to the power workers' union which was urging the power rebels to go back. Instead of this, he was demanding that the men concerned should be paid while they were working to rule. Joe Ashton, Benn's assistant who resigned over the way the dispute was handled (not by Benn, for whom he had great admiration) called in the debate on the affair initiated by the Opposition, for the Government to lean heavily on the electricity industry bosses. In the end the strike was called off because of the singularly hostile public reaction — some of the strikers were even spat upon when they went to supermarkets to shop.

The miners were out to grab £135 a week in blatant defiance of the pay code. The Coal Board offered a rather phoney but face-saving productivity deal which the miners rejected. What did Benn do at this juncture? He went to visit a coal pit at Newton-le-Willows, taking care to have himself photographed in overalls and with his face covered in coal, dust and grime. To some it looked as if he was trying to identify himself with the miners' pay claim. In the end the miners did swing round in favour of the productivity deal but because of Joe Gormley, the NUM President, rather than Benn, who refused to speak in favour of it until positively ordered to do so by Callaghan. As Terence Lancaster asked in the *Daily Mirror*:

> 'Is Mr. Benn actively disloyal?
> Certainly not.
> Is he passively disloyal?
> Well, that's another question.'

Even these important matters concerning Benn's own department were not the only causes for dispute with his leader. He clashed with Callaghan and Party Secretary, Ron

Hayward, in a Transport House Meeting on 22 November 1977 over a proposal which they favoured for a series of private opinion polls to be taken in the run up to the election and which were to cost £150 000. Benn argued in stentorian tones that such devices were 'useless'. The outcome was that the Committee decided to spend only £50 000. That at least might be dismissed quite literally as a matter of opinion, but in January 1978 there was another row when Labour's campaign committee shelved plans to allow the Trotskyite-dominated Young Socialists to produce a party political broadcast for television. It was going to be an out and out class war broadcast, all about the rich shopping in Harrods and holidaying in the Bahamas and living in £100 000 houses and featuring an interview with Benn. Callaghan was clearly worried at the time that the young Trots' broadcast, coming before the Ilford by-election, would blow the gaff on what the Labour party was really like, and that the public would not care for it.

Benn was finding himself more and more out of favour. By March 1978, Callaghan was actually talking about how the left wing should drop their reflationary ideas and listen to what ordinary people wanted, which was reductions in tax. Nothing could be more in conflict with the ideas of a large increase in public spending of Benn and his chums on the NEC.

The lesson of this detailed account of Benn's protracted conflict first with Wilson and then with Callaghan over his desire to push party policy to the far left and meeting with a resistance virtually never on grounds of principle, but purely with an eye to what the electorate would accept, is that Benn and the radical ideas for which he stands are now very powerful, too powerful for him to be sacked, despite repeated threats, as long as he does not push defiance too far. Even such a vague qualification may not be justified now, because on several occasions Callaghan, who is not one to brook opposition kindly, has been humiliated by the decisions of Benn and the NEC, and never more blatantly than when it confirmed the appointment of Andy Bevan. It is this power to defy the leader and Prime Minister with near impunity, rather than his lack-lustre performance as Minister of Energy, which has made Benn appear increasingly formidable in this latest phase of his career. Approve of him or not, he is a figure in British politics whom we are at least compelled to take seriously.

11
MAN OF DESTINY?

In a speech to a closed meeting in Carlton House Terrace in September 1977 Benn asserted that history was moving his way. All the big reforms, he said, took place in Britain in forty year cycles — 1832 and 1867 (Reform Bills); 1906 (reforming Liberal government); 1945 (reforming Labour government). On that basis Britain was due for a 'great leap forward' in a few years' time. And the implication as to who would be the leader to carry through the new era of reform, if left hanging in the air, was also never in doubt. Naturally it was that great apostle of democracy and equality, none other than Benn himself! Of course the encapsulated history course was not everybody's idea of how to chart the growth of progress and reform. Indeed 1906 (when trades unions became legally immune) and 1945 (the first big bout of nationalisation) would to some look like milestones on the road to serfdom and to our nation's economic and political decline. It would certainly be the fit culmination of such a trend to have Benn as Prime Minister in 1984!

However, confidence in one's own destiny is a vital, often *the* vital, element in success. Why should this be a bad thing? Is Benn so manifestly the wrong man to trust with the fate of this country? Why should he be worse than any of the other possible Labour leaders, if, elections being what they are, we are obliged to have a Labour leader a couple of Parliaments' on?

Certainly the danger of Benn is not that he is himself an evil, unprincipled or malignant individual. Most people who have known him personally agree that he is a man of unusual amiability and charm, buoyant in spirit, resilient in bad times as well as good, amusing, stimulating and witty. Among politicians, who seem as a profession to be excessively afflicted with marital troubles, he stands out as the very model of a happy family man. Admittedly there is something of the eccentric about him. His habit for instance of drinking twenty pints of tea every day from a suitably proletarian tin mug sets him apart from most of his colleagues in the House (though quaintly enough it puts him in the same league as Brigitte Bardot, who drinks eighty cups of tea a day while filming). Martin Walker of the *Guardian* discovered that the drug in tea, caffeine, was used to dope horses in the 'twenties, but since discarded. When he rang up the Jockey Club to ask why, he was told, 'The drug is far too uncertain in its effects. It by no means guarantees a fast run. Sometimes they just stand there and froth at the mouth.' Still, eccentricity within wide limits is not going to be much of a handicap to ambition in Britain where, if anything, it is an advantage. Benn's quirks and occasional bizarre antics which arouse little more than wry amusement, have their importance in that they lead people to dismiss him as something of a buffoon.

Nothing could be more mistaken than to laugh him off in this way. For his political skills are of a high order: he is a gifted speaker, a tireless campaigner and an assiduous and powerful committee man. As an MP he is energetic and by current standards, according to which a member tends to be valued for his ability to command special treatment for his constituents from government departments and in particular to speed up for them the provision of the goodies of the Welfare State, he is remarkably good — at least to judge by a study done by Frances Morrell, his political adviser, of his constituency work during the year 1972. He has also swayed vital decisions. In 1973-74 Benn was for a time practically in charge of the Labour party and almost single-handedly by cajolery and persuasion lined up the Shadow Cabinet behind the miners when Wilson had lost his nerve, thus bringing about the defeat of Heath and Labour's return to power. It was, one former colleague said sardonically, Benn's finest hour. But this was only the culmination of a steady drive from within the Labour party organisation where he had become, as he remains, well established. As a leading member of the National Executive and as Chairman of the home affairs committee, he can radicalise not only policy but in almost Stalinist fashion the party cadres — as in his successful instalment of the Trotskyist Andy Bevan as Labour's Youth Organiser in defiance of his leader and Prime Minister.

It is as well to appreciate Benn's virtues and strengths because if he were merely the raving lunatic that some take him for then the danger he constitutes to our society would perhaps be past. For it is at times of crisis that people who are actually demented do rise to the top and Benn's demand that the British economic crises from 1974 on should be regarded as the opportunity for transforming society might be thought to be in keeping with his role as a budding Robespierre. Equally the fading of the immediate prospect, once very real, of bankruptcy and runaway inflation might suggest a fading of Benn's political prospects too. To think so however would be a mistake because even when the crises are over Benn's power base in the Labour party will remain. So well placed is he that if there were an election tomorrow for leader at the Labour party conference, he would sweep to power.

If Benn is not to be discounted as a mere fanatic whose time has come and gone, he is not to be pigeonholed and set aside as scheming cynic either. Like most people his is a mixture. In one aspect — and this accounts for a good deal of the sympathy as well as the scorn which he evokes — he is a naive idealist, a happy warrior, a wide-eyed boy scout or a do-gooding crusader. At the same time he is the political manipulator, the calculating opportunist, in many respects sincere, but always the most sincere in his ambition. This can of course be entirely honourable; it is perhaps the particular element which gives an element of grandeur to the political struggle, raising it above the level of triviality to which it can so easily fall. But given too free a rein, ambition can distort all the values and lead to inconsistency and hypocrisy. This is especially the case with Benn because of his mercurial temperament. He is apt to respond to an idea which is put to him at one moment with boundless enthusiasm. How disconcerting if he responds with equal fervour a moment or two or even a week later to an idea of a totally different kind! There are journalists like this in Fleet Street, some famous names among them, who are not hypocrites, but who are capable of writing passionately on opposite sides of a question literally within the same week. This is partly because they over-emphasise journalistic values — asking is this view interesting rather than is it right or true — and Benn, who considers himself in the professional sense to be a journalist, to some extent shares this mentality. It also argues a certain ideological rootlessness, a deficiency of philosophic grasp and a lack of ultimate conviction. Such people may look strong, assertive and in command of their own destiny, but in reality they are often easily influenced by fashions in ideas, the advocacy of other articulate people, or by chance events. Such volatility of course becomes all the more pronounced in those who yearn for popular approval — in Benn's case with the peculiarity that, as an admirer sadly observed, 'He doesn't like leading, but he does like being followed'.

This at least is how it seems reasonable to account for the numerous inconsistencies between many of Benn's views and his behaviour, and between many of the views themselves. We need not dwell on the strange flight into fantasy on the occasions already mentioned when he has attempted to suggest that his origins were more lowly than they actually were. No doubt his romantic attachment to the idea of himself as a working-class leader temporarily overwhelmed his respect for facts: what Freud calls his super-ego (proletarian hero) was stronger than his reality principle. He is also inclined to repaint, or anyway touch up, his family background. For instance, in an article in *The Times* about his late father, William Wedgwood Benn, who had been born a century before, he recalled his father's elevation to the Lords: 'It had to be a hereditary peerage, since life peerages did not then exist'. Yes, but as Norman Lamont MP pointed out in a letter at the time, a hereditary peerage need not have entailed more than a mere barony: his father was created a Viscount! His article also mentioned his grandfather, John Benn, who first went to work in the City as an office boy at the age of eleven in his mother's boots, but forebore to mention that he was rewarded for his public services in 1914 with a baronetcy! It is amusing to recall that Benn, who was himself such a reluctant Viscount and has grown increasingly vituperative in his demands for disarming and eventually abolishing the House of Lords, strongly urged Fenner Brockway to accept a peerage after he lost his seat at Slough in the general election of 1964. This may have been prompted by kindness, but it does suggest that perhaps his hostility to the Lords was emotive rather than principled, more a case of titles being all right as long as they were conferred on his friends.

It is one of Benn's affectations, at least when electioneering, to wear the sort of clothes which identify him with the workers whose votes he seeks. As a Minister he is constantly photographed in shirtsleeves. His most recent sartorial initiative of note was a miner's overalls, tin hat and grimy face. Such gestures of solidarity with his supporters are not objectionable but understandable, especially when we remember the myth of betrayal of Labour voters by Ramsay Macdonald, who would address a meeting of the unemployed as his 'working class friends' his evening dress suitably draped in an overcoat, and then hurry off, excusing himself for having to attend to important government business, but in fact in order to adorn a ball at Lady Londonderry's. There is a point nevertheless at which the attempt to demonstrate that there is no difference between the rulers and those who put them there turns into humbug — it was rumoured that Nye Bevan would go down to Wales in a limousine and then a little short of his constituency transfer to a Morris Minor. Those who preach equality should practise it, and some do: apparently when R.H. Tawney went to America to lecture on socialism he insisted on travelling third class, whereas Lord Lindsay, Master of Balliol, who was with him travelled first. Perhaps that underlined the difference between two kinds of socialist. However, impractical, Tawney was the one who commanded respect.

In this context, what undermines the credibility of Benn is the contrast between the quiet opulence of his life-style — a £70 000 house in Holland Park, a fine and secluded family retreat in Stansgate Abbey House, near Southminster, Essex, where his mother lives, and which can only be reached down a two mile long private road — and his close connection with the class war political broadcasts for the Labour party put on by his former assistant, Joe Ashton. Is he not of the same class as the programme's imaginery target, the Hon. Algernon, who started life with a silver spoon in his mouth? And if the anger of the workers is to be provoked, as it was to be in the banned broadcast by Andy Bevan's Young Socialists, against those who could afford to spend £1000 at the drop of a hat in Harrods or holiday in the Bahamas, then is not his exceedingly rich American wife, Caroline, just the sort of person at whom the programme was aimed? If it is all right for Tony Benn to live in affluence then it is all right for city stockbrokers to live that way too. Humbug is proferring a lofty moral standard and living by another considerably less lofty. Benn has no business allying himself with those who denounce the privilege which he enjoys. In this respect he is just another public school socialist assaulting the 'system' which gave him such a start in life and the fruits of which he still consumes.

Still, personal humbug or peccadilloes have little direct

effect on the way the country is ruled and apparently small effect on the voters either, who seem to remain almost wilfully ignorant of the private lives of leading politicians. As an example, until he announced it to the world in a posthumous book, how many of the public realised that Tom Driberg was a practising homosexual? And is it conceivable that he would have gone on being returned at general elections had it been general knowledge? Yet this was known to everybody else at Westminster and the current joke when he was raised to the peerage was that it was for 'services to cottage industries'. This conspiracy of silence about the personal lives of our rulers may be a good thing in many ways, but it is particularly helpful to those socialists who preach about equality and live the life of Riley, or at least the high-toned Hampstead life of Peter Simple's Mrs. Dutt-Pauker. Let it be clear that there is no wish here to condemn people for adopting, at least within very wide limits, what life-style they please. What is surely unacceptable is censoriousness towards other people doing the same thing.

More important than gaps between public and private standards, as far as the public interest is concerned, are the conflicting political values for which Benn has stood, though whether he is fully conscious of the contradictions is not easy to determine. An instance of this was when he said about the dockers imprisoned under the Industrial Relations Act, 'If a man's conscience lands him in jail, the bars that keep him there also imprison a part of all our freedoms'. Nobly said, one might think, but these men were simply acting to defend their economic privileges against other workers. Their troubles were derisory compared with those of the men who by their hundreds have lost their jobs in nationalised industries because of their refusal to join a union. This much greater infringement of freedom of conscience has not yet produced the slightest response from Benn. Why do his moral qualms dry up when trades union interests are involved?

Benn took his stand and campaigned first of all alone and then with overwhelming success on the need to consult the

people through a referendum on the question of whether
Britain should remain a member of the Common Market.
The reason for this departure from the normal British
practice of making political decisions through Parliament
was that joining the Community was an 'irreversible' decision
'which would transfer certain powers from the British
parliament to the EEC'. That was perfectly reasonable, but if
the principle of popular consent through referendum applied
to joining the EEC, it should apply to other areas of policy
too. Consider Labour's election manifesto of February 1974
which committed the party to 'bring about a fundamental
and irreversible shift in the balance of power and wealth in
favour of working people and their families'. The wording,
to judge from previous speeches of Benn's, was very likely
his. Yet, an 'irreversible' decision like this surely needed
specific popular affirmation through a referendum. After all,
irreversibility implies no second chance just as much in the
case of changing the power structure of British society as it
does in the case of joining the EEC. This programme was
only accepted, and even then only as part of a larger package,
by 37.2 per cent of those who voted and by less than 30 per
cent of the electorate. Would we not therefore expect Benn to
be in favour of having a referendum on this question? Nor
can he really defend himself on the grounds that a shift of
power in favour of working people and their families would
necessarily appeal to the majority, because in practice what
Labour offers are only changes which their policy-makers
interpret as being in favour of working people and their
families — nationalisation, or reserving work exclusively for
dockers on both of which there is evidence that the mass of
working people is less than enthusiastic. And there are many
other areas of policy such as hanging, immigration, and the
closed shop where Benn has shown not the least inclination to
consult the people through the referendum process. One is
therefore drawn to the conclusion that Benn's belief in
decision-making by the people is so selective as to amount to
nothing more than an expedient judged according to its

usefulness in helping Benn's career, or at least promoting those causes he attaches himself to at any one time.

The classic example of Benn's volatility has been in his changing attitude to Europe. If we begin in 1963 with his contribution to a symposium on the EEC in *Encounter* he was then opposed to the Community because 'the Treaty of Rome — which entrenches *laissez-faire* as its philosophy and chooses bureaucracy as its administrative method — will stultify effective economic planning without creating the necessary supra-national planning mechanism for growth and social justice under democratic control'. By 1967 when Wilson was applying for membership and spouting about a Technological Community (big role for Benn at Min Tech?) these objections had been forgotten. After the 1970 election the main thrust of his argument was that the people should decide either way through a referendum, his opposition only growing as Labour turned against entry in 1971-2. When the referendum came down two to one in favour of staying in, he unequivocally accepted it. By June 1977 however he was on the move again, and made a speech saying that Britain could still leave the Common Market. Only a month before that, he had written an article about his father, quoting the latter's admirable belief that 'we do not choose our convictions, but they choose us and force us to fight for them to the death'. In his son's case, especially as regards Europe, conflicting ideas seem to have advanced and retreated like the dancers in a minuet. All these shifts seem to owe nothing to principle and almost everything to fluctuations in public opinion and the tactical situation.

Indeed, the one thread which runs constantly through Benn's belief is audience appeal. Although he likes to pose as a philosopher, and, as a friend of earlier days said 'he gives this curious impression of depth' he is above all else a populist. He has the mentality of a demagogue and the temperament of a rhetorician and a romantic. This has much to do with his rather gaseous performance as a Minister. As we have seen, especially in his periods at the post office, (more new telephones instead of better service) and at the Ministry of Energy (conference-mongering instead of decision taking, and Christmas handouts to old age pensioners) he is apt to spend his time and effort on those things which are most for show, or which most easily present the greatest opportunities for propaganda, or which bring a fast electoral return, rather than meeting the objective needs of the sector or people concerned. Similarly at the Ministry of Technology the foci of his interest were sci-fi toys like the hovercraft and the electric car which were hardly central to what Min Tech was supposed to be about. Worse still both at Min Tech and at the Energy Ministry his populist inclinations led him to beat the nationalist drum in technological matters, whereas the most important thing he could have done in each Ministry was to ensure that Britain made the best of the technology available on the international market, the proportional contribution to which of one country, even Britain's, would necessarily be small.

Again Benn's love of instant popularity has been pretty disastrous as far as his economic decisions have been concerned because it led time and again to the short-term preservation of jobs in lame duck outfits like Upper Clyde Shipbuilders at the expense of the rest of the industry. Upper Clyde's uneconomic wage rises made the rest of shipbuilding unprofitable and by adding to the tax burden of still viable firms elsewhere in the economy put other workers out of a job. This illustrates the classic weakness of the corporate state: it is apt to surrender and give privileges to the most vociferous and best-orchestrated pressure groups at the expense of the majority. Thus the paradox is that populism, when in control of the economic levers of the state — especially the leviathan which the socialism of all parties has landed us with today — is not helpful to the mass of the people, but only to the minority who have learned how to milk it.

However, Benn is not a populist for all seasons, for he necessarily operates within limits, not only those imposed by the nature of the Labour party, but also those emanating from the radical tradition of his family and especially his father, by whom he was greatly influenced, which has been reinforced by his wife's radical chic — seemingly a characteristic of American women who marry British socialist politicians! Consistent or not, and whether primarily regarded as crusader or politician on the make, the fact remains that Benn, however he may gyrate in future, stands for a recognisable programme today. He took the trouble to spell that programme out when he was making his not over-serious attempt to be elected Labour's leader in March 1976. It came under these three headings:

1. *A siege economy*

   He would pursue a policy of full employment by import controls combined with expansion, partly generated by higher government spending (with certainly no limits on public sector borrowing or the money supply) and direction of investment, partly through nationalised industries and through planning agreements in the private sector.

2. *Open government*

   He would restore to Parliament and the people the capacity to control government, Whitehall and the public corporations by a major exercise in open government and an extension of the power of MPs.

3. *Industrial democracy*

   Essentially this would be the adoption of the Bullock recommendations for worker directors on company boards, or more likely given Benn's general outlook, Bullock plus, with worker directors in the majority on boards.

The siege economy proposals alone would guarantee

Britain's growing impoverishment. The removal of restraints on public spending would, to go by experience alone, produce runaway inflation which would in turn create the excuse for more and more economic controls and burgeoning bureaucracy producing no doubt for a time full employment of a kind — with half of the population being paid to watch the other half. The idea that British industry would become more competitive by removing foreign competition is of course absurd, since the only restraint now left against sloppy British workmanship is that the consumer can buy from abroad. Direction of investment will not help either since, as the series of disasters promoted by Benn himself suggests — Court Line, Meridan, the *Scottish Daily Express,* to mention only a few — central government is considerably worse at investment than the private sector and its failures drain the resources of such profitable sectors of the economy as remain. We need not be impressed either by the fact that Benn's views about economic management derive from, or coincide with, those of the Cambridge School whose members, though clever theoreticians, hold a disastrous record in practice, since it is largely the Keynesians of Cambridge in Whitehall who have been in charge of the British economy since the war. In any event, as Schumpeter said of similar types in his day, though they appear to be talking about economics they are really talking radical politics.

In his plea for open government, Benn shows his customary flair for recognising an important issue, for there is growing impatience with Whitehall's secrecy. Yet, while there can be no objection to extending the power of MPs to bring public bodies, Ministers and officials increasingly to account, the rest of his programme would multiply enormously the amount of government activity to be supervised. Surely the first task in bringing government under the control of the people is to reduce the scale of government to the point where it becomes comprehensible and manageable.

As for industrial democracy, anything like the Bullock proposals would produce the exact opposite — a syndicalist despotism. Bullock would not put worker representatives on the board but nominees (often not even from the workplaces concerned) of the union bosses. Even this might be workable if, as in West Germany, the unions broadly supported the capitalist free enterprise system but needless to say, neither Benn nor most of Britain's union leaders do. So we would have, in many cases, communists and Trotskyists in the boardroom regarding it as their duty to prevent the firm making profits and to bring it down in ruin as soon as possible so that the next stage, the socialist revolution, could proceed without delay. Even if in some way their wrecking proclivities could be confined, the effect of the Bullock/Benn type scheme would be to hand over British industry bound and gagged into the hands of the union chiefs.

Benn's blueprint for Britain would indeed produce the worst of all worlds. It would create a kind of Soviet economy, but bereft of the iron discipline that holds that misbegotten system together. It would obviously mean the end of free enterprise or even any approximation to free enterprise which can be described as a mixed economy. Few have put the point better than Ernest Benn, the late uncle of the subject of this book, in his best-seller *Confessions of a Capitalist:*

'I am an unrepentant believer in free enterprise. I have failed to discover, in a long and diligent search, any material benefit which has ever reached mankind except through the agony of individual enterprise. I therefore regard the whole movement for creating wealth through political agencies as a snare and a delusion. For these reasons I see no essential difference between the Bolshevik of Russia and the numerous types of moderate socialist ... I am reminded of two murderers who filled a good many newspaper columns a year or so ago... Both directed their attentions to the same victim.

The method of the one was to administer small doses of ground glass. The other adopted the more straightforward and direct method of the dagger. The moderate socialist is the groundglass practitioner; the communist is the dagger. But insofar as they are both bent on the abolition of private enterprise they are both murdering the chances of the human race to achieve a higher standard of comfort.'

There is more than comfort at stake, however, as Sir Ernest was powerfully aware. His nephew would also affirm that more important by far are the values of democracy and freedom. Yet history is our witness that only the system of capitalist free enterprise has so far created the political pluralism — that is the dispersion of power throughout society — by which alone democracy and freedom are sustained.

If Tony Benn's life to date means anything, it is that given the power, he would not so much carelessly as with relish destroy that system and those values. That is why if the warning of this book goes unheeded and in the course of years he is allowed by the electors to take charge of Britain's destinies, the only hope must be a meagre one — that Benn's behaviour from that point on will not be consonant with his past.

INDEX